"My Rosary"

An Exorcist's Beloved Prayer

"My Rosary"

An Exorcist's Beloved Prayer

by Gabriele Amorth

Translated by
Bret Thoman

Icona Press
Peachtree City, Georgia

My Rosary: An Exorcist's Beloved Prayer
by Gabriele Amorth

Cover design by Angie Alaya.
Cover image by kropekk_pl.

Originally published as: Il Mio Rosario
© 2016 Edizioni San Paolo s.r.l.
Piazza Soncino, 5 - 20092 Cinisello Balsamo (Milano) – Italia
www.edizionisanpaolo.it

English translation by Bret Thoman, OFS
English edition copyright © Bret Thoman. 2023

Published by Icona Press.
www.stfrancispilgrimages.com

ICONA PRESS
IMITATE THE SAINTS

I dedicate this book to the Immaculate Heart of Mary, on whom the future of our world depends, as revealed through the messages of Fatima and Medjugorje. In 1917, Our Lady prophesized the eventual triumph of her Immaculate Heart by saying, "In the end, my Immaculate Heart will triumph.

And coming to her, he said,
"Hail, favored one! The Lord is with you."

(Luke 1:28)

Table of Contents

Translator's Note

When I discovered this book, published by San Paolo Edizioni in Italy, I knew I had to translate it. Fr. Gabriele Amorth was considered one of the most important figures in the Italian Catholic Church. After his death in 2016, at the age of 91, his work and ministries have become all the more compelling. The recent Hollywood film about his life (though highly embellished) has only added to the mystique.

During my work on this translation, I discovered that behind the man was a powerful faith. He could not have worked for thirty years as an exorcist without supernatural aid. Toward the end of his life, retired in a rest home in Rome, he revealed his secret: the Rosary.

For years, he had an unpublished book that he kept hidden in a drawer of his cell in the Generalate of the Paulines in Rome. It consisted of reflections and meditations on the rosary that he wrote personally. This is what gave him strength to fight against the devil for three decades. Shortly before he died, he gave it to his order to publish.

Fr. Amorth was a noted theologian and biblical exegete. As a biblical scholar, he breaks open all twenty mysteries of the Rosary one by one. Using scriptural passages, papal teachings, and biblical research, Fr. Amorth brings these mysteries to life.

After I read this book, I have not prayed the Rosary in the same way. It is my hope that this book, brief but compact, will be a light to you, as well.

Lastly, I would like to thank the following people for their collaboration: Fr. James Blount, SOLT, reader; Angela Moulpied, editor; Anita Barretto, editor; Gina Avila Marhevka, editor; and Cathy Smith, editor.

Introduction

I believe that, after the Holy Mass and the Liturgy of the Hours, the rosary is the most powerful prayer. This is evident from the various writings of several popes, including Pope St. Pius V and onward, which I have summarized in the first appendix.

I would like to mention that Pope St. John Paul II filled a void in the ancient prayer of the rosary. It had been believed for a long time that the rosary contained the entirety of the Gospel. However, this wasn't entirely true, as the public life of Jesus was not contemplated as a Mystery. The rosary jumped from the fifth Joyful Mystery (the Finding in the Temple) to the first Sorrowful Mystery (the Agony in the Garden). With inspiration from the Most Holy Virgin, Pope John Paul II introduced the Luminous Mysteries. Added after the Joyful Mysteries, these mysteries summarize the entirety of the public life of Jesus.

In this book, I have presented the reflections that I recite daily on the twenty mysteries. My hope is that they will be useful to those who recite the rosary and meditate on the mysteries.

THE JOYFUL MYSTERIES

(Monday and Saturday)

1: The Annunciation

(THE FIRST JOYFUL MYSTERY)

In the sixth month, the angel Gabriel was sent from God to a town of Galilee called Nazareth, to a virgin betrothed to a man named Joseph, of the house of David, and the virgin's name was Mary. And coming to her, he said, "Hail, favored one! The Lord is with you." But she was greatly troubled at what was said and pondered what sort of greeting this might be. Then the angel said to her, "Do not be afraid, Mary, for you have found favor with God. Behold, you will conceive in your womb and bear a son, and you shall name him Jesus. He will be great and will be called Son of the Most High, and the Lord God will give him the throne of David his father, and he will rule over the house of Jacob forever, and of his kingdom there will be no end." But Mary said to the angel, "How can this be, since I have no relations with a man?" And the angel said to her in reply, "The holy Spirit will come upon you, and the power of the Most High will overshadow you. Therefore the child to be born will be called holy, the Son of God. And behold, Elizabeth, your relative, has also conceived a son in her old age, and this is the sixth month for her who was called barren; for nothing will be impossible for God." Mary said, "Behold, I am the handmaid of the Lord. May it be done to me according to your word." Then the angel departed from her. (Luke 1:26-38)

God prepared the two individuals whom he entrusted his Son to very carefully. The fruits of Christ's redemption were anticipated in Mary at the moment of her conception, which is why she was born without original sin, and is therefore known as the Immaculate Conception. According to tradition, Mary consecrated herself entirely to God, making her the perfect example of an "ever-virgin" woman. It is worth noting that in the Jewish culture, there are no similar instances of women choosing to remain celibate. Prior to Jesus' teachings, the Jewish people only honored motherhood, as infertility was considered a disgraceful condition. In addition, people hoped to one day be related to the Messiah, but Mary's decision to remain a virgin would have ended that possibility. It is also important to mention that Mary was married to Joseph, making Jesus a member of a family.

Joseph, too, was well-prepared by God for his role in Jesus' life. First and foremost, he was a "righteous" man, meaning that he was completely devoted to and receptive to God. Additionally, he was a member of the family of David. Once recognized as Joseph's son, Jesus became a legal descendant of David, and could rightfully be called the "son of David." Lastly, Joseph was a blacksmith-carpenter, which gives us insight into the economic circumstances in which Jesus grew up. While it would have been a modest environment, they were not impoverished.

The marriage took place in two stages. In the first stage, the bridegroom would have declared, "I take Mary as my wife, according to the law of Moses," in the presence of their parents and two witnesses. This declaration constituted a valid marriage, even if the newlyweds still lived with their respective families for some time. The second stage of the marriage involved a celebration that typically lasted for seven days, after which the bride would be brought into the house that the bridegroom had prepared.

Mary was troubled by the angel's greeting. Instead of the common greeting, "Shalom," which means "peace to you," Gabriel used the word "Chaire" (Χαῖρε) in Greek, which is translated as "Hail" in English. This word means "exult," "be happy," and "rejoice," and is a well-known term used only once by three prophets (Zechariah, Zephaniah, Joel) in a messianic context. Mary was left wondering what connection there could be between herself and the Messiah. Additionally, the angel did not address her by name but instead referred to her as "favored one" and said, "the Lord is with you." The words of this salutation confused Mary, and she pondered the significance of such a greeting.

Gabriel then explained to Mary about her future motherhood, her son's name, which means "God is salvation," and his eternal Kingdom, all of which indicated that he was the awaited Messiah. While Mary believed with simplicity, she also felt overwhelmed by her own insignificance. The only question she asked was how all of this was going to take place.

Gabriel gave her a complete answer: everything will be done by the work of the Holy Spirit. That is, it will be a miraculous birth, similar to other well-known births in Israel. Despite facing other difficulties, Mary trusted wholeheartedly in her Lord. She gave her unconditional consent by declaring herself as the handmaid of God.

After Mary gave her consent, the Holy Spirit intervened, and the Word of God was made flesh. This is why we celebrate the Incarnation of the Word on the day of the Annunciation. March 25 is the day of the announcement, which takes place nine months before Christmas, which in turn falls on December 25.

2: The Visitation

(THE SECOND JOYFUL MYSTERY)

During those days Mary set out and traveled to the hill country in haste to a town of Judah, where she entered the house of Zechariah and greeted Elizabeth. When Elizabeth heard Mary's greeting, the infant leaped in her womb, and Elizabeth, filled with the holy Spirit, cried out in a loud voice and said, "Most blessed are you among women, and blessed is the fruit of your womb. And how does this happen to me, that the mother of my Lord should come to me? For at the moment the sound of your greeting reached my ears, the infant in my womb leaped for joy. Blessed are you who believed that what was spoken to you by the Lord would be fulfilled."

And Mary said: "My soul proclaims the greatness of the Lord; my spirit rejoices in God my savior. For he has looked upon his handmaid's lowliness; behold, from now on will all ages call me blessed. The Mighty One has done great things for me, and holy is his name. His mercy is from age to age to those who fear him. He has shown might with his arm, dispersed the arrogant of mind and heart. He has thrown down the rulers from their thrones but lifted up the lowly. The hungry he has filled with good things; the rich he has sent away empty. He has helped Israel his servant, remembering his mercy, according to his promise to our fathers, to Abraham and to his descendants forever." (Luke 1:39-55)

Mary pondered over the words of the angel, who had told her that the birth of her child would be miraculous. Gabriel had used the example of a miraculous conception in a barren woman. But instead of citing well-known figures like Sarah, the wife of Abraham, he referred to Mary's relative, Elizabeth. This led Mary to realize that there was a connection between her child and Elizabeth's. Furthermore, Gabriel mentioned that Elizabeth was in her sixth month of pregnancy. This may have been to emphasize that Elizabeth, in her old age, would need assistance during the final three months of her pregnancy.

Elevated by God to a unique greatness and feeling acutely aware of her own smallness, Mary felt a strong need to serve. Six months earlier, Gabriel had revealed God's plan by announcing the birth of John. Mary perceived the relationship between these two announcements and hastened to the place where God's plan was set in motion.

The encounter between Mary and Elizabeth has two "hidden" protagonists: the sons they are both carrying in their wombs. The greeting that Mary addresses to her elderly cousin is simple. I believe she would have said, "Shalom" (peace to you). This sends the Holy Spirit upon Elizabeth, who exclaims loudly, "Most blessed are you among women, and blessed is the fruit of your womb. And how does this happen to me, that the mother of my Lord should come to me? For at the moment the sound of your greeting reached my ears, the infant in my womb leaped for joy. Blessed are you who believed that what was spoken to you by the Lord would be fulfilled."

This is a powerful response that reveals a complete revelation of the Holy Spirit to Elizabeth. The first fruit of Mary's simple greeting is the joy with which John leaps for joy in his first encounter with Jesus. These are the two protagonists of the visit. However, it is Elizabeth who is the first to recognize that the child in Mary's womb is the Lord; that is, her God.

Elizabeth was the first person to call Mary "Mother of God." She was also the first to acknowledge Mary as "most blessed among women." Centuries later, St. Francis of Assisi would address Mary in a prayer, saying, "There is no one like you." It is important to note that Elizabeth praised Mary for her faith, saying "Blessed are you who believed," as Elizabeth had experienced the disappointment of her husband Zechariah's lack of faith, which left him mute until the birth of their son John (see Luke 1:20-22).

These are the four "firsts" that establish Elizabeth as a remarkable prophetess of the New Testament. Without hesitation, I refer to her as such because she speaks with divine inspiration. Elizabeth is truly moved by the Holy Spirit.

After hearing Elizabeth's words, Mary responds with the beautiful hymn of the Magnificat. It is the only instance where Mary speaks at length, and she uses this opportunity to praise God's power and mercy. In her exaltation of the heavenly Father, Mary exclaims, "My soul proclaims the greatness of the Lord; my spirit rejoices in God my savior. For he has looked upon his handmaid's lowliness." There is also a sense of gratitude in her words, as she feels saved and lifted up from her lowliness to the highest summit, above all humanity.

Mary's statement, "all ages [will] call me blessed," begs the question why. She acknowledges that she is nothing, but the Mighty One has done great things for her, and his name is holy. Mary explains that God's power lies in the rebirth of all humanity, as he lifts up the lowly and casts down the arrogant. The proud are scattered, rulers are thrown down, and the rich are sent away empty-handed. Conversely, the lowly are lifted up, and the hungry are filled with good things. Mary's words anticipate the spirit of the Sermon on the Mount, when Jesus pronounces the beatitudes.

Finally, Mary praises God for his faithfulness to the promise made to Abraham and his descendants forever, who were spread throughout the world, saying, "In you all nations will be blessed." He fulfilled this promise by sending the long-awaited Messiah. Jesus is the heir and fulfillment of those promises. With him, the new people of God begins, extended to all nations, and concretized in the Church.

3: The Nativity of Our Lord
(THE THIRD JOYFUL MYSTERY)

In those days a decree went out from Caesar Augustus that the whole world should be enrolled. This was the first enrollment, when Quirinius was governor of Syria. So all went to be enrolled, each to his own town. And Joseph too went up from Galilee from the town of Nazareth to Judea, to the city of David that is called Bethlehem, because he was of the house and family of David, to be enrolled with Mary, his betrothed, who was with child.

While they were there, the time came for her to have her child and she gave birth to her firstborn son. She wrapped him in swaddling clothes and laid him in a manger, because there was no room for them in the inn.

Now there were shepherds in that region living in the fields and keeping the night watch over their flock. The angel of the Lord appeared to them and the glory of the Lord shone around them, and they were struck with great fear. The angel said to them, "Do not be afraid; for behold, I proclaim to you good news of great joy that will be for all the people. For today in the city of David a savior has been born for you who is Messiah and Lord. And this will be a sign for you: you will find an infant wrapped in swaddling clothes and lying in a manger." And suddenly there was a multitude of the heavenly host with the angel, praising God and saying: "Glory to God in the highest and on earth peace to those on whom his favor rests."

When the angels went away from them to heaven, the shepherds said to one another, "Let us go, then, to Bethlehem to see this thing that has taken place, which the Lord has made known to us." So they went in haste and found Mary and Joseph, and the infant lying in the manger. When they saw this, they made known the message that had been told them about this child. All who heard it were amazed by what had been told them by the shepherds. And Mary kept all these things, reflecting on them in her heart. (Luke 2:1-19)

God sometimes uses circumstances or events that appear to be random or coincidental to fulfill his plans. In the case of Joseph, who was from the house of David, he had to travel to Bethlehem not because he knew that the prophecy of Micah predicted that the Messiah would be born there, but because he was required to do so by the Roman government's census. Mary, who was pregnant at the time, accompanied Joseph on this journey, even though it was inconvenient and uncomfortable, because she was obedient to the civil authorities and to her husband. Despite the contingent motives that led Joseph and Mary to Bethlehem, God used this journey to fulfill his plan of having Jesus born in the city of David, according to the prophecy.

The holy couple arrived in Bethlehem around the time of the birth of their child. However, it was not convenient for them to stay in the caravanserai–the roadside inns along the caravan routes where travelers usually took refuge. Such a situation, with so much commotion, would not have been appropriate. Nor would they have been comfortable if they had accepted hospitality in a private home or with Joseph's own family. In that era, it was customary for all the members of a family to sleep together in a single room.

The holy couple felt most comfortable taking refuge in a grotto, which was likely used to shelter animals in case of rain. They may have chosen the best cave, one that was deep enough and therefore better sheltered. The cave was probably equipped with a long manger dug into the rock at the bottom and along the width of the cave. This would have provided space for storing their belongings and served as a crib for the newborn child. It is not surprising that the Son of God was born in what we would refer to as a hovel, given the poor conditions in which his family lived.

Jesus was born. I believe that at that moment, Mary felt the greatest joy of her life. She kissed her baby, swaddled him, placed him in the manger, and contemplated him. Together with Joseph, they were ecstatic and determined to dedicate their lives entirely to him. Mary understood more and more how God had prepared her for this moment, the purpose of her entire existence.

The first visitors who came to pay their respects to Jesus were not the rich, but the shepherds. These were the poorest and most unfortunate people, who were often considered "second class" citizens. Shepherds were believed to be unreliable and bent on stealing. They were not allowed to serve as judges, and their testimony was not considered trustworthy in trials. However, God chose to send his angel to announce the great news to these shepherds: "For today in the city of David a savior has been born for you who is Messiah and Lord. And this will be a sign for you: you will find an infant wrapped in swaddling clothes and lying in a manger."

The shepherds immediately understood everything. They knew that the city of David was Bethlehem, and if the child was lying in a manger, it meant that he was the long-awaited Messiah with a unique relationship with God, but he was also extremely poor. He was born in a cave with a manger as his crib. The shepherds wasted no time and went to honor the child. Mary and Joseph were pleased with the visit of the poor shepherds, who gave them no cause for concern. As the shepherds recounted how they had been told by the angel, Mary and Joseph rejoiced once again at the ways of God. He had chosen the poorest to receive the great announcement.

The poor understand each other well and are always willing to help those who are even less fortunate than themselves. It's probable that when the shepherds departed, they left some cheese or milk-based products for the Holy Family, who had nothing at that moment. This act of kindness was truly providential. Furthermore, the shepherds spread the joyous news among the people.

The narrative concludes with a significant observation: "Mary kept all these things, reflecting on them in her heart." While others might be inclined toward action, Mary tended toward contemplation. It is possible that Luke wanted to reveal the source of this event. In fact, in the prologue to his Gospel, Luke mentions that he began writing after carefully investigating everything from the beginning. This included consulting eyewitnesses, as he mentions earlier. At the time Luke when was writing in Jerusalem, only Mary knew all the details regarding Jesus' infancy. Therefore, they could have only been recounted by her.

4: The Presentation

When eight days were completed for his circumcision, he was named Jesus, the name given him by the angel before he was conceived in the womb. When the days were completed for their purification according to the law of Moses, they took him up to Jerusalem to present him to the Lord, just as it is written in the law of the Lord, "Every male that opens the womb shall be consecrated to the Lord," and to offer the sacrifice of "a pair of turtledoves or two young pigeons," in accordance with the dictate in the law of the Lord.

Now there was a man in Jerusalem whose name was Simeon. This man was righteous and devout, awaiting the consolation of Israel, and the holy Spirit was upon him. It had been revealed to him by the holy Spirit that he should not see death before he had seen the Messiah of the Lord. He came in the Spirit into the temple; and when the parents brought in the child Jesus to perform the custom of the law in regard to him, he took him into his arms and blessed God, saying:

"Now, Master, you may let your servant go

in peace, according to your word,
for my eyes have seen your salvation,
which you prepared in sight of all the peoples,
a light for revelation to the Gentiles,
and glory for your people Israel."

The child's father and mother were amazed at what was said about him; and Simeon blessed them and said to Mary his mother, "Behold, this child is destined for the fall and rise of many in Israel, and to be a sign that will be contradicted (and you yourself a sword will pierce) so that the thoughts of many hearts may be revealed." (Luke 2:21-35)

The childhood of Jesus adhered to the customs prescribed for Jewish children during that time. Eight days after his birth, he was circumcised to confirm his belonging to God's chosen people. During this occasion, he was named Jesus, as revealed by the angel. Forty days later, he was presented in the temple as a ransom, and his mother underwent the rite of purification.

The ransom of Jesus had a different meaning from the purpose for which the rite was instituted. In commemoration of the sparing of the firstborn in Egypt, it was believed that the firstborn of the Israelites belonged to God and needed to be redeemed. However, for Jesus, there was no need for redemption. His parents presented him to God in obedience, fully aware that he already belonged entirely to the Father. Moreover, his mother, who had entirely offered herself to God, was united with her son in this recognition. Furthermore, God united Joseph and all humanity with himself. God knew that he had sent his Son to reconcile humanity and bring all people back to him. He lovingly accepted Mary's complete offering.

Then came the brief ceremony of purification. Here, too, we find Joseph associated with Mary, although only Mary was required for this rite, which consisted of a simple prayer. Joseph was seen to take part, as long as he was alive, in what happened through Mary and through Jesus. On this occasion, the holy couple presented the prescribed offering of two doves, which was the offering of the poor. If they had been wealthy, they would have offered a lamb or a kid.

At this point, an unexpected figure is introduced. Surely, the elderly Simeon must have shared with Joseph and Mary that the Spirit had revealed to him that he would not die until he saw the Christ of the Lord, and that the same Spirit had led him to the temple. It was evident to Mary and Joseph that he was a prophet, and they willingly entrusted the infant Jesus into his arms.

Simeon gazed upon the infant with immense love and proclaimed, "Now, Master, you may let your servant go in peace, according to your word, for my eyes have seen your salvation." He then added a prophecy that warrants contemplation, stating that the child would be the "salvation of all peoples"–a light for all, not just for Israel but for everyone, as God promised Abraham, saying, "All the families of the earth will find blessing in you" (Genesis 12:3).

Then changing his tone, he declared that Jesus would be a sign of contradiction for those who listened to him and for those who rejected him, and that he would bring about resurrection for some and downfall for others. Turning to the Mother, he added, "And you yourself a sword will pierce, so that the thoughts of many hearts may be revealed." Mary's life would be marked by the piercing of a sword. The sword symbolized not only an instrument of killing, but also of division. Mary's soul would feel the division of hearts–those who accepted the salvation of Christ and those who rejected it, even to the point of condemning Jesus.

These words were a painful revelation for Mary. She then realized that the life of Jesus would not be a constant triumph, as the promises of Gabriel on the day of the Annunciation suggested; these "glories" would come later. She also understood her role better. It was not limited to the birth and childhood of Jesus; instead, she would be his disciple for her entire life, through all the sufferings, until the end. Faced with this anticipation, Mary gave her complete "yes," just as she had given her "yes" to becoming the Mother of Jesus. Thus, Mary remains a model for us of continuously saying "yes" to God— in joy and in pain.

5: The Finding in the Temple

(THE FIFTH JOYFUL MYSTERY)

Each year his parents went to Jerusalem for the feast of Passover, and when he was twelve years old, they went up according to festival custom. After they had completed its days, as they were returning, the boy Jesus remained behind in Jerusalem, but his parents did not know it. Thinking that he was in the caravan, they journeyed for a day and looked for him among their relatives and acquaintances, but not finding him, they returned to Jerusalem to look for him. After three days they found him in the temple, sitting in the midst of the teachers, listening to them and asking them questions, and all who heard him were astounded at his understanding and his answers. When his parents saw him, they were astonished, and his mother said to him, "Son, why have you done this to us? Your father and I have been looking for you with great anxiety." And he said to them, "Why were you looking for me? Did you not know that I must be in my Father's house?" But they did not understand what he said to them.

He went down with them and came to Nazareth, and was obedient to them; and his mother kept all these things in her heart. (Luke 2:41-51)

The law required every able-bodied Israelite to visit the temple of Jerusalem three times a year–during Passover, Shavuot (Pentecost), and Sukkot (Feast of Tabernacles). Those who lived more than one day's walk away were exempt from this obligation. For example, going from Nazareth to Jerusalem would have taken four or five days. Despite being exempt, Mary and Joseph went to Jerusalem every year for Passover.

Luke narrates the story of Jesus being lost and then found in the temple as a significant event in the total mystery of Christ and as a foreshadowing of his ultimate fate on the cross. As a result, he presents this event as the most important episode during Jesus' hidden life in Nazareth.

In Jerusalem, Jesus deliberately separates himself from his parents and enters the temple, driven by his obedience to a higher authority–that of his Father, who will guide him throughout his life. At the temple, he begins to exhibit the characteristics that will define his preaching: he engages in bold disputes with the scribes and Pharisees, he faces judgment and death but ultimately triumphs in his Resurrection, and from Jerusalem, he will eventually ascend to the Father, completing the circle of his divine mission.

The details of Jesus getting lost make sense with some knowledge of the customs of that time. During Passover, many Jewish caravans traveled to Jerusalem. As they approached the holy city, the caravans grew larger and more people joined. On the return journey, the phenomenon was the opposite: initially, many large caravans left Jerusalem in groups, stopping overnight before continuing their journey. As some people reached their destination and others went in other directions, the caravans dwindled in size and number. As a result, it was not possible to know who was present or missing until arriving at the first overnight stop. At that point, Mary and Joseph waited for the other groups, hoping that Jesus was in one of them.

Mary endured an agonizing wait, longing to see her son after a long and tiring day. Several groups arrived without him, causing her distress. She spent a terrible night wondering where Jesus was. The next day, Mary returned to Jerusalem with her anxiety and uncertainty still looming. Another sleepless night full of questions followed. On the third day, there was a great sigh of relief as she saw Jesus healthy and radiant speaking in the temple. It is impossible to consider this without seeing it as an allusion to the Passion–loss, death, three days of harrowing waiting that resembles the sepulcher, and a cry of joy upon finding, which symbolizes the Resurrection. Luke must have had these references in mind while writing about this event.

The Messianic significance of the event is highlighted by Mary's question and Jesus' response: "Son, why have you done this to us? Your father and I have been looking for you with great anxiety." It is noteworthy that Luke uses the same word to describe the pains of Hell when referring to Mary's great anxiety. Those were truly hellish hours for the parents of the child. Perhaps Mary was asking if there was a specific reason for Jesus' actions and what he would do now that he was about to become an adult (which occurred at the age of thirteen in the Jewish custom). Who knows how many questions Our Lady asked during that painful period of darkness?

Jesus' response to his parents' search for him is his first words handed down in the Gospels. These words hold such vast meaning that they couldn't be understood right away: "Why were you looking for me?" This response was not a reproach, but rather a way for Jesus to make himself understood. In his words, there is a reference to the sacrifice of the cross, when the angels will say to the women who go to the tomb: "Why do you seek the living one among the dead?" (Luke 24:5). Jesus then goes on to say, "Did you not know that I must be in my Father's house?" In other words, Jesus meant that when he was forty days old, he was offered entirely to the Father.

There are three points to underline:

1. "that I must be…" Obedience to God is an imperative duty and superior to obedience to parents.

2. "in my Father's house…" What concerns God is contrasted with what concerns the parents.

3. "My Father…" In response to "your father," mentioned by Mary. This comparison does not demean Joseph, but recalls reality and the absolute precedence that belongs to God.

We should add that the joy of being found after three days is a foreshadowing of the Easter joy, when Jesus rises again on the third day. The suffering of Mary and Joseph recalls the agony of Mary, the apostles, and the devout women due to the Passion and death of Jesus. It seems that Jesus' response, which is filled with prophetic references, only becomes clear after the events he was predicting take place.

Another teaching that I am eager to point out from Jesus' comportment is that we must not hesitate to respond to God's invitations. The Lord speaks to each one of us in various ways, such as through our temperaments, life's opportunities, and the examples of others. He even calls us in exceptional situations, and in those cases, the Lord expects a prompt and definitive response. In the Gospel, we have the example of the rich young man who refuses Jesus' call, leading to deep reflections on wealth. (See Matthew 19:16-30.)

The Gospels contain other significant examples, such as those who expressed a desire to follow Jesus but wanted to bury their dead first. Jesus refused them, rejecting those who wished to follow him but also wanted to say goodbye to family members. In my opinion, Jesus foresaw how many vocations would be lost due to attachment to one's family. He also saw how many religious vocations would be cut short by the pull of family needs. Whoever gives himself to God cannot look back.

Jesus understood the suffering he had caused Mary and Joseph very well. He recognized it immediately and returned with them to Nazareth, where he obediently lived with them for many years.

The episode ends with a remark from Luke that "his mother kept all these things in her heart." It appears that the repetition of this remark, which is identical to what was written after the visit of the shepherds to Bethlehem, serves not only to delve into Mary's inner life but also to confirm the identity of the person who reported these details to him in such a detailed manner.

THE LUMINOUS MYSTERIES

(Thursday)

6: The Baptism in the Jordan
(THE FIRST LUMINOUS MYSTERY)

Then Jesus came from Galilee to John at the Jordan to be baptized by him. John tried to prevent him, saying, "I need to be baptized by you, and yet you are coming to me?" Jesus said to him in reply, "Allow it now, for thus it is fitting for us to fulfill all righteousness." Then he allowed him.

After Jesus was baptized, he came up from the water and behold, the heavens were opened [for him], and he saw the Spirit of God descending like a dove [and] coming upon him. And a voice came from the heavens, saying, "This is my beloved Son, with whom I am well pleased." (Mt 3:13-17)

It is truly wondrous to witness how Jesus begins his public ministry as a Teacher and as the Way, the Truth, and the Life. He travels from his hometown of Nazareth in the Galilee region to Judea, where John the Baptist is baptizing in a secluded place near the banks of the Jordan River. Despite his sinlessness, Jesus humbly joins the line of sinners, already with his feet immersed in the river, ready to receive a baptism of repentance.

When it was Jesus' turn to be baptized, John couldn't contain his amazement. We do not know for sure if Jesus and John had met before this moment. However, John's mother had likely informed him about the extraordinary character of Jesus and Mary. As the one who prepared the way for Jesus, John could not help but express his astonishment, saying, "I need to be baptized by you, and yet you are coming to me."

But Jesus responded, "It is fitting for us to fulfill all righteousness." In other words, Jesus believed that receiving a baptism of penance from John was the right thing to do in order to fulfill God's plan.

How can this be? Because Jesus came to save the world from its sins. How did he do this? By bearing on his shoulders all the sins of humanity, from Adam to the last person who will live on earth. He is the true Lamb of God, who takes upon himself all the sins of the world and transforms sinners into children of God.

Let's reflect on this: Our sins are already completely forgiven before God through Jesus. For Catholics to receive forgiveness, they must sincerely repent of their sins, forgive anyone who has offended them, and confess. (As for people of other faiths, there are ways that only God knows, such as sincere repentance and love of neighbor.) St. Paul said it clearly and concisely: "For our sake he made him to be sin who did not know sin" (2 Corinthians 5:21). Therefore, it is right that he, the most innocent, should submit to a baptism of penance.

At this point, we can only admire the total humility of Jesus as he takes on the condition of sinners and unites himself with them before John the Baptist. It is precisely here that God the Father, in communion with the Holy Spirit, who appears in the form of a dove, intervenes with his voice. This is one of the great theophanies. In response to Jesus' act of humility, a resounding affirmation is heard: "This is my beloved Son, with whom I am well pleased."

With this, the first act of Jesus' life comes to a close. He withdraws into the desert to confront and defeat his mysterious enemy, Satan.

7: The Miracle at the Wedding of Cana

(THE SECOND LUMINOUS MYSTERY)

On the third day there was a wedding in Cana in Galilee, and the mother of Jesus was there. Jesus and his disciples were also invited to the wedding. When the wine ran short, the mother of Jesus said to him, "They have no wine." [And] Jesus said to her, "Woman, how does your concern affect me? My hour has not yet come." His mother said to the servers, "Do whatever he tells you." Now there were six stone water jars there for Jewish ceremonial washings, each holding twenty to thirty gallons. Jesus told them, "Fill the jars with water." So they filled them to the brim. Then he told them, "Draw some out now and take it to the headwaiter." So they took it. And when the headwaiter tasted the water that had become wine, without knowing where it came from (although the servers who had drawn the water knew), the headwaiter called the bridegroom and said to him, "Everyone serves good wine first, and then when people have drunk freely, an inferior one; but you have kept the good wine until now."

Jesus did this as the beginning of his signs in Cana in Galilee and so revealed his glory, and his disciples began to believe in him. (John 2:1-11)

This is a beautiful image. At the beginning of his public life, Jesus sets out to take part in a wedding and sanctify the family. He works his first miracle on behalf of this family who was certainly not wealthy, as there was not enough wine to last for the duration of the feast.

The wedding celebration would have lasted for seven days, as it was customary to honor the definitive introduction of the bride into the home of the bridegroom. The guests would not have arrived empty-handed, but would have brought animals, bread, sweets, and whatever else was needed for the long celebration.

Mary arrived early, possibly as a relative of the bride or groom, and may have come to assist with preparations. She demonstrated a degree of authority by giving an order to the servants. Jesus was also invited to the wedding, along with his early apostles, and likely arrived at the beginning of the celebration. It should be noted that not all guests participated in the full seven days of festivities and there was some amount of coming and going.

After a few days, Mary realized that the wine had run out, which would have been an extraordinary problem. It would have interrupted the wedding celebrations and seriously humiliated the newlyweds. This is why Mary quickly intervened with her son, saying, "They have no wine." Then, Jesus gave a puzzling response to biblical scholars when he said, "Woman, how does your concern affect me? My hour has not yet come."

"Woman": Jesus already sees his Mother through the perspective of the Kingdom of God, which has been opened up to him. Mary is no longer just his earthly mother; rather, she has a fundamental role in the New Testament. She is the Woman who was already announced in Genesis as the Mother of the new humanity. She is the conqueror of Satan, united with her Son to crush the head of the serpent. She is the new Woman, crowned Queen of Heaven and Earth, in the final Kingdom where Jesus is the High King, so that it may be clear that Jesus is the only mediator between God and man.

However, for his work to reach all people, Jesus needs us. His first cooperator is Mary, followed by the apostles, parents who educate their children in the faith, parish priests, missionaries, and all those who pray and offer up their sufferings in union with the crucified Christ. St. Paul writes, "I have been crucified with Christ" (Galatians 2:19) and "I am filling up what is lacking in the afflictions of Christ on behalf of his body, which is the church" (Colossians 1:24). All Christians are called to be, after Mary, collaborators in the redemption.

The other words that Jesus said to Our Lady seem very clear if one assumes that some things had been said between Mary and Jesus during the long period of their life together in Nazareth. Jesus prepared the apostles on several occasions by foretelling his dramatic Passion and death, followed by his Resurrection on the third day. I believe he prepared his Mother even more, and with more details, by announcing their separation of three years during which they would not even speak to each other, and giving her a time at "the hour," that is, at the moment of his death at the foot of the cross. With these assumptions, Jesus' response makes sense. Mary understood her son's words as a response to what he had already told her; that is, "at the moment at the foot of the cross." She also understands that he is not refusing to intervene regarding the lack of wine. For this reason, she says to the servants, "Do whatever he tells you.

This authoritative invitation from Mary is of the utmost importance, as it underscores her role as a key intercessor between humanity and her Son, Jesus Christ. Moreover, they are her last words recorded in the Gospels, and they serve as a testament to all people for all times. Even in Marian apparitions recorded in the history of the Church, all of Mary's words repeat the same invitation to do everything Jesus said, even if we do not understand some things right away. This highlights the importance of obedience to Jesus, as demonstrated by Mary's unwavering faith and trust in her Son's will.

Various levels of astonishment followed. First, the servants were amazed when Jesus instructed them to fill six jars with water, with capacities of 80 or 120 liters. Mary's admonition to "Do whatever he tells you" was helpful in encouraging them to carry out the task, even though they did not understand the reason behind it. Similarly, they were puzzled as to why they were supposed to give the headwaiter a taste of the water.

Then there was amazement on behalf of the headwaiter at drinking such good wine when the wedding feast was so far along. He said to the groom, "Everyone serves good wine first, and then when people have drunk freely, an inferior one; but you have kept the good wine until now."

Finally, the guests were also amazed when they found out that there was an abundance of excellent wine, drawn from the jars of water. Jesus' gift was truly supernatural, as there were approximately 600 liters (160 gallons) of excellent wine. There was enough to last until the end of the festivities and some left over. People were curious about the origin of the wine, and the miracle performed by Jesus came to light. This way, Jesus was glorified, and people began to discover who he really was. The apostles' trust in the Master they followed also increased.

8: The Proclamation of the Kingdom of God

(THE THIRD LUMINOUS MYSTERY)

I begin this chapter, which I have divided into four parts, with a premise. Various popes, especially from Leo XIII onwards, have declared that the rosary allows us to meditate on the entirety of Jesus' life. However, his entire public life was missing. We note that only the third Luminous Mystery summarizes all of Jesus' preaching. The first two lead us to contemplate the beginning of Jesus' public life: his baptism in the Jordan and the miracle at Cana, while the final two mysteries present us with two important events: the Transfiguration and the institution of the Holy Eucharist.

With that, I will focus on the third mystery by delving into a verse from the Gospel of Mark, which introduces the preaching of Jesus in four phrases. He begins his evangelization by saying: "This is the time of fulfillment. The kingdom of God is at hand. Repent and believe in the gospel" (Mark 1:15).

Phrase One: "This is the time of fulfillment." The sin of our progenitors, Adam and Eve, led to a great victory for Satan. But the coming of a woman was foretold, whose Son would crush the head of Satan, who had presented himself in the guise of a serpent (see Genesis 3:15). This is known as the famous "proto-gospel"—the first announcement of salvation, which opened up a great period of waiting.

Who will this woman be? Above all, who will this child be? Who will overcome Satan and annul the underlying causes of original sin? When God decided it was time to prepare for the coming of this child, he created a people into which he would be born. The father of this people was Abraham. From him, the people of Israel would come forth.

The tribe of Judah—one of the twelve tribes descended from the sons of Jacob—was chosen for the birth of this child. Among the families of this tribe, the family of David was appointed. At this point, the expectation of the promised Savior—that is, the Messiah—was increasingly felt urgently. It was believed that the Messiah would be a great general, like David, who would fight and win numerous battles throughout his reign. Thus, they believed that the Messiah would free the people of Israel from the yoke of the Romans and make the kingdom of Israel invincible above all nations.

When Jesus announces that the time is fulfilled, the time of waiting is understood as finished. There is no longer any need to wait for the Messiah, because the Messiah has come. Jesus did not say, "I am the Messiah." In this regard, biblical scholars refer to what is known as "the messianic secret." Jesus kept the fact that he was the Messiah a secret. He imposed silence on those who knew who he was because the people were expecting the establishment of a military kingdom. Instead, the Kingdom of God, which Jesus inaugurates, is something completely different.

Phrase Two: "The kingdom of God is at hand." His was not a political realm, but a spiritual one. Jesus initiates a new Kingdom, open to all peoples, as God had already predicted to Abraham when he said, "All the families of the earth will find blessing in you" (Genesis 12:3). The first to enter this Kingdom, which begins with the public mission of Jesus, is Mary, Most Holy. For this reason, Jesus refers to her as "woman" in that moment. She is the woman foretold in Genesis, whose Son would defeat Satan.

Another narrative of Jesus is telling. While preaching to a crowd of people in a house, someone said to him, "Your mother and your brothers are standing outside, asking to speak with you" (Matthew 12:47). He replied, "Who is my mother? Who are my brothers?" (48). Then he stretched out his hand toward his disciples and said, "Here are my mother and my brothers. For whoever does the will of my heavenly Father is my brother, and sister, and mother" (49-50). In this way, he shows the new family that he is creating. It is not a conquering army, as the Jews believed the Messiah's army would be. Instead, by founding and leading the Kingdom of God, which is aimed at all people, Jesus wants to show everyone how to love one another and get to Heaven.

Phrase Three: "repent" (that is, "conversion"). This concept has expanded greatly in today's context. While we often associate this term with an atheist or someone from another religion becoming Christian, or a non-practicing, baptized Catholic returning to Mass and the sacraments, the meaning of the word goes beyond that. Essentially, to repent or convert means to change one's mentality. Therefore, Jesus constantly exhorts everyone to convert, which we will explain further. (This is also the message of Our Lady of Medjugorje).

The primary and foundational change in one's mentality is to recognize that our time in this world is limited, and that we are meant for eternal life. Too often, we become consumed with worrying about the problems of this world, as if we will be here forever. But the truth is that our time on earth is short, even if we were to reach the age of 120 like Moses. What lies ahead is an eternal life that never ends. The quality of our eternal life will depend on how we prepare for it in this earthly life. It can be stupendously beautiful or horribly disastrous. Therefore, we must shift our focus from the temporary concerns of this world to the eternal perspective. We must strive to live our lives in a way that leads us toward the ultimate goal of everlasting happiness.

I frequently meet parents who are overwhelmed and discouraged by their children's misbehavior. When I ask them if they provided their children with physical nourishment, they answer yes. But when I ask if they also fed their children's souls, they are often unsure. It is important to remember that children have a spiritual side that requires attention and nurturing. Parents have a unique opportunity to teach and guide their children until the age of ten or eleven. After that, their peers and environment often have a stronger influence. However, it's never too late to make a positive impact. Children are naturally receptive to prayer, love for Our Lady and Jesus, and goodness. They just need to be shown the way.

According to Sacred Scripture, we were created through the Word of God and for Jesus Christ (Colossians 1:16). Jesus is the reason for our existence and the purpose for which we live. There is no greater goal than Jesus Christ and the eternal happiness of Heaven that he invites us to share in. Keeping our minds focused on this fundamental truth can put the various ups and downs of life into perspective. As the Catechism of Pius X asks, "Why did God make man?" The answer is simple: "To know him, to love him, and to serve him in this world, and to be happy with him forever in heaven." These thoughts should guide and inspire us as we journey through life.

Conversion is a lifelong process because we will always have areas in our lives where we can grow and improve. Moreover, the Lord sets before us an extraordinary goal: "Be perfect, just as your heavenly Father is perfect" (Matthew 5:48). This is not an attainable goal in this life, but rather a goal toward which we should strive. It reminds us to never be satisfied with our current state of being and to recognize that the journey ahead of us is much longer than the one we have already traveled. Even the saints, who made great strides in their spiritual lives, still had imperfections and flaws at the time of their death. Whether they did not notice them or did not have time to overcome them, they remind us that spiritual growth is a continual process that requires a lifetime of effort.

"Repent!" This invitation is for everyone. All of us will constantly have to strive to progress in our imitation of Jesus.

Phrase Four: "believe in the gospel." With this declaration, Jesus inaugurates his preaching and calls on all to listen to it and accept it. Many of Jesus' teachings are summarized in his final days when he declared, "I give you a new commandment: love one another. As I have loved you, so you also should love one another" (John 13:34). This is a new commandment because it surpasses the ancient and still relevant commandment to "love your neighbor as yourself." Jesus presents himself as the ultimate model of love, having loved us so profoundly that he gave his life for us. As St. John teaches us, we too must love one another to the point of sacrificing ourselves for our neighbor.

On this journey, the first step is humility, which means always having an attitude of humble understanding: "Take my yoke upon you and learn from me, for I am meek and humble of heart" (Matthew 11:29).

A second step is to serve others, as Jesus himself stated: "For the Son of Man did not come to be served but to serve" (Mark 10:45). Thus, Jesus teaches us to always place ourselves last.

A third step is to serve in humility. An excellent example of this is when Jesus washed the apostles' feet and said: "If I, therefore, the master and teacher, have washed your feet, you ought to wash one another's feet" (John 13:14). Although foot-washing is not a common practice today, we should still accept humiliations to express our love for our neighbors. For example, a mother's or a wife's love for her family may involve selfless service and humility.

The fourth step is to give one's life for one's neighbor. This is what Jesus did, and it is what many missionaries, parish priests, educators, and family members still do when they sacrifice their lives for others. The evangelization of Jesus is full of other examples that are necessary for salvation, such as heartfelt forgiveness, which is the condition for being forgiven by God. Another example is loving our enemies, which is required by our religion and can be heroic at times. This is charity in all its applications. Finally, fundamental in this regard is the universal judgment presented to us in Matthew 25. The preaching of Jesus has so many treasures that we must listen to and follow.

9: The Transfiguration
(THE FOURTH LUMINOUS MYSTERY)

After six days Jesus took Peter, James, and John his brother, and led them up a high mountain by themselves.

And he was transfigured before them; his face shone like the sun and his clothes became white as light. And behold, Moses and Elijah appeared to them, conversing with him. Then Peter said to Jesus in reply, "Lord, it is good that we are here. If you wish, I will make three tents here, one for you, one for Moses, and one for Elijah."

While he was still speaking, behold, a bright cloud cast a shadow over them, then from the cloud came a voice that said, "This is my beloved Son, with whom I am well pleased; listen to him."

When the disciples heard this, they fell prostrate and were very much afraid. But Jesus came and touched them, saying, "Rise, and do not be afraid." And when the disciples raised their eyes, they saw no one else but Jesus alone. As they were coming down from the mountain, Jesus charged them, "Do not tell the vision to anyone until the Son of Man has been raised from the dead." (Matthew 17:1-9)

The Transfiguration is a pivotal event in the life of Jesus. The Lord wanted the testimony of three privileged apostles whom he had called close to him at other times. This is the only occasion during his earthly life in which Jesus essentially lifted the veil of his humanity, revealing the splendor of his divine nature. He did so in the presence of two authoritative representatives of the Old Testament: Elijah, who represents the prophets; and Moses, the great legislator who sanctioned the first covenant between God and the people of Israel.

I remember visiting the high mountain of Mt. Tabor in the Holy Land, identified by tradition as the site of the Transfiguration. Upon arrival, a bus drops you off at a parking lot located below the steep slopes, where you wait for local taxis to take you up to the top via switchbacks. The summit is dominated by a solemn basilica that commemorates the Transfiguration. It was on this mountain that the three apostles witnessed the resplendent face of Jesus and his luminous clothing. They felt a joy and happiness they had never experienced before emanating from him. It was truly a spectacle of Heaven, and the three apostles did not want to leave. This is why Peter responded spontaneously, almost without thinking, that they build three tents. However, he was later ashamed, recognizing that this idea was impossible to carry out.

The three apostles witnessed Jesus in his glorified state, as he would appear after the Resurrection. This event served a clear purpose: Jesus wanted to prepare them for the sight of him disfigured during his Passion. By showing them his permanent beauty, he hoped they would remember it even when it was temporarily marred by the torture he endured until his death on the cross.

In the Gospel narrative, there is no mention of what was spoken between Jesus, Moses, and Elijah. St. Luke says only that they spoke of his "exodus"; that is, his imminent death (see Luke 9:31). This means that the Transfiguration has a very close connection with the most disconcerting event of the entire Gospel: the death of Jesus. Therefore, the Transfiguration would serve to strengthen the faith of the disciples during that moment of crisis.

Suddenly, a luminous cloud—a sign of God's presence—interrupted everything, and a divine voice was heard: "This is my beloved Son, with whom I am well pleased; listen to him." These were almost the same words that were heard after Jesus' baptism in the Jordan River, although at that time the voice was only heard by Jesus and possibly by John the Baptist. Here, all three apostles clearly heard the voice, and they were amazed, particularly by the command to "listen to him."

Their fear was so great that they fell face down and could not find the strength to stand up. Jesus approached them, touched them, and said, "Rise, and do not be afraid." They stood up and saw only Jesus, in his usual appearance, with no sign of Elijah or Moses. As they descended the mountain, Jesus warned them not to tell anyone about what they had seen until after the Son of Man had been raised from the dead. It was a difficult command to obey, as they longed to proclaim to the world what they had witnessed.

But there was something else that disturbed them and was difficult to understand. They were instructed to keep quiet until Jesus rose from the dead. But they had no idea what that meant. When Jesus spoke about the Resurrection, it was apparent that he was talking about something totally foreign to their experience.

It's true that Jesus had tried to prepare them by pre-announcing his horrific Passion, crucifixion, and death, followed by his Resurrection on the third day. Surely, these were painful and greatly troubling words. The disciples didn't want to accept this, and they didn't dare ask for a clearer explanation.

Yet, there was something else that made Jesus' words even more confusing. In the Old Testament, there was no concept of a resurrection to eternal life. When a "resurrection" occurred by the work of a prophet, it was only a return to one's earthly life, as one had left it, to die a natural death at a later time. Such cases could be better defined as a "miraculous return to life." They meant living again or returning to one's earthly life. The Resurrection of Christ is something entirely different. He did not return to his earthly life in the way he was before his death. Instead, he was resurrected with an immortal body that possessed altogether different qualities, allowing him to encounter eternity. This difference justifies the apostles' difficulty in understanding Jesus' words. They realized that when he spoke of Resurrection, he meant something different from those resurrections they may have heard of or even witnessed, as in the case of Lazarus or the daughter of Jairus.

For us, it is clear what Jesus meant when he spoke of his definitive Resurrection, upon which the definitive resurrection of our bodies at the end of times depends. At that time, we too shall encounter eternal life.

10: The Institution of the Holy Eucharist

(THE FIFTH LUMINOUS MYSTERY)

"I am the bread of life. Your ancestors ate the manna in the desert, but they died; this is the bread that comes down from heaven so that one may eat it and not die. I am the living bread that came down from heaven; whoever eats this bread will live forever; and the bread that I will give is my flesh for the life of the world."

The Jews quarreled among themselves, saying, "How can this man give us [his] flesh to eat?"

Jesus said to them, "Amen, amen, I say to you, unless you eat the flesh of the Son of Man and drink his blood, you do not have life within you. Whoever eats my flesh and drinks my blood has eternal life, and I will raise him on the last day. For my flesh is true food, and my blood is true drink. Whoever eats my flesh and drinks my blood remains in me and I in him. Just as the living Father sent me and I have life because of the Father, so also the one who feeds on me will have life because of me. This is the bread that came down from heaven. Unlike your ancestors who ate and still died, whoever eats this bread will live forever."

These things he said while teaching in the synagogue in Capernaum. (John 6:48-59)

This harsh discourse caused many of Jesus' followers to leave him, as John narrates in the following dialogue: "Jesus then said to the Twelve, 'Do you also want to leave?' Simon Peter answered him, 'Master, to whom shall we go? You have the words of eternal life. We have come to believe and are convinced that you are the Holy One of God'" (John 6:67-69). Even the other apostles agreed with Peter in recognizing that Jesus, the Son of God, had their full trust, no matter what he said. But now and then, in discussions amongst themselves, they may have asked what he meant when he said, "my flesh is true food, and my blood is true drink." Among other things, the Jews considered it repugnant to consume blood. If they came across a strangled animal, they were to leave it there to be eaten by wild animals. They believed that blood was the center of the soul and held that all souls should return to God.

Thus came the great day of the Last Supper, and all the apostles understood that Jesus considered this event to be exceptionally important. He knew of a large hall with tables and recliners for solemn meals that could be used, and he assigned two apostles to prepare the supper. The Jewish Passover supper was not a large meal, but rather a meticulously prearranged liturgical function in the form of a supper. Everything from what to eat, where and how to sit, and the prayers to be recited were carefully prescribed.

We note that there are four narratives regarding the Institution of the Holy Eucharist: those of Matthew, Mark, Luke, and St. Paul. John's account is absent because he wrote his Gospel last. Knowing that the three synoptic Gospels had already covered the subject, he chose not to rewrite what they had already written. Instead, he aimed to convey other aspects of Jesus' life and teachings. Therefore, he did not write about the institution of the Eucharist, but instead focused on the great discourse in which Jesus foretold it, which we read at the beginning of this chapter.

At a certain point during the supper, Jesus becomes solemn and poised, and all fall silent with their eyes fixed on him. He takes the bread, breaks it, gives thanks, and says, "Take and eat; this is my body" (Matthew 26:26; see also Mark 14:22). He then adds solemnly, "which will be given for you; do this in memory of me" (Luke 22:19; see also 1 Cor 11:24). The apostles silently passed a piece of the bread to each other. As they tasted it, they realized that it had the flavor of unleavened bread, which was traditionally used by the Jews at paschal meals. However, they were also certain that it was no longer just bread; it was much more. They pondered over the words "given for you" and reflected on how Jesus gives himself and dies for others, as St. Paul would later express, "Jesus loved me and died for me" (Galatians 2:20).

Once again, at the end of the supper, Jesus becomes serious. He takes the large chalice of wine, gives thanks, and declares, "This cup is the new covenant in my blood, which will be shed for you" (Luke 22:20). The apostles take a sip and pass the cup to one another. Although the wine has the familiar flavor, they know that it contains much more than the fruit of the vine. Then, his words were clear, "my flesh is true food, and my blood is true drink." By giving himself to us in the form of common food and drink, he unites us to himself.

After hearing Jesus' words about the new covenant, the apostles reflected on their significance. They recognized that the old covenant, which was established through the shedding of animal blood and governed the relationship between God and the Jewish people, had come to an end. Now, a new and eternal covenant had begun between God and all people, based on the gift that Jesus made of his entire life. This new covenant was definitive and offered the promise of salvation to all who would accept it.

As the apostles contemplated the meaning of Jesus' blood shed for them and for all, they came to understand that he had taken upon himself all the sins of the world—past, present, and future—and had obtained forgiveness for all through his blood. They realized that the only thing required for this pardon, which had already been secured, was to apply it to individual persons. For Catholics, this takes place through repentance, forgiving those who have offended us, and sacramental confession. (For others, it may happen based on conditions known by God.)

With the words, "Do this in memory of me," Jesus bestowed tremendous power upon the apostles. The principal role of priests is to offer sacrifices to God. By giving the apostles the power to offer this sacrifice, Jesus communicated his priesthood to them. Therefore, on Holy Thursday, we commemorate both the Institution of the Holy Eucharist and the Institution of the Priesthood.

Before ascending to Heaven, Jesus promised, 'I am with you always, until the end of the age' (Matthew 28:20). The Eucharist is one way in which the Lord has kept his promise, despite knowing the risks it would be subject to. The first risk is that of disbelief. To counter this difficulty, Jesus permitted Eucharistic miracles throughout the world. The foremost Eucharistic miracle is that of Bolsena, which involves a corporal (linen) that was bloodied during Mass and is preserved today in the splendid cathedral of Orvieto. This miracle led to the institution of the feast of Corpus Christi.

A second risk is that of loneliness. Jesus anticipated that he would spend many hours shut up in a tabernacle or in a closed or abandoned church. St. Therese of the Child Jesus said that if Christians truly believed in the Eucharist, all the churches in the world would always be full, with the need for personnel to regulate the comings and goings of the faithful.

A third risk is the most painful: Jesus allowed so many communions that there could be sacrilegious Eucharistic celebrations. Worse still, Jesus knew that Eucharistic hosts would be stolen, and there would be other outrages against the sacred species, including the wicked abuse of the Eucharist perpetrated by satanic sects, especially during black masses.

But none of this discouraged Jesus. He saw that the Eucharist would be at the center of the entire liturgy of the Church. He would witness innumerable devoted communions. He saw that the Eucharist would sustain countless souls and inspire many apostolates. He also saw that there would be religious communities, churches, and parishes that would organize Eucharistic adoration day and night. Therefore, he didn't give up in the face of the possibility of wicked deeds.

After reciting this fifth mystery, I believe that we should spend at least some time in Eucharistic Adoration.

THE SORROWFUL MYSTERIES

(Tuesday and Friday)

11: The Agony in the Garden
(THE FIRST SORROWFUL MYSTERY)

Then Jesus came with them to a place called Gethsemane and he said to his disciples, "Sit here while I go over there and pray." He took along Peter and the two sons of Zebedee, and began to feel sorrow and distress. Then he said to them, "My soul is sorrowful even to death. Remain here and keep watch with me." He advanced a little and fell prostrate in prayer, saying, "My Father, if it is possible, let this cup pass from me; yet, not as I will, but as you will."

When he returned to his disciples he found them asleep. He said to Peter, "So you could not keep watch with me for one hour? Watch and pray that you may not undergo the test. The spirit is willing, but the flesh is weak."

Withdrawing a second time, he prayed again, "My Father, if it is not possible that this cup pass without my drinking it, your will be done!"

Then he returned once more and found them asleep, for they could not keep their eyes open. He left them and withdrew again and prayed a third time, saying the same thing again. (Matthew 26:36-44)

After the Last Supper, Jesus goes to the Garden of Gethsemane at the bottom of the Mount of Olives, a short distance away. However, during this brief journey, a radical transformation takes place within him. He feels oppressed by fear and dejection, to the point where he says, "My soul is sorrowful even to death. Remain here and keep watch" (Mark 14:34). From that moment until his death, Jesus feels alone.

At a certain point, Jesus stops the disciples and urges them to keep watch with him in prayer. He especially recommends this to Peter, James, and John, whom he wants even closer to him. Then he lies face down on the ground and prays for a long time, saying, "My Father, if it is possible, let this cup pass from me; yet, not as I will, but as you will."

In his prolonged prayer, Jesus teaches us some important lessons about how to pray. Here are three reflections:

1. It is appropriate to pray for our material needs, such as health, work, and emotions. However, we must remember that if we do not go beyond this, we are not really praying, but just making requests. Prayer is much more. The first step is to adore the Lord, who is so great and holy. The second step is to thank him for all that we are and have, recognizing that everything is a gift from him and not due to our own merit. The third step is to ask him for forgiveness for our failings. Then, the last step is to ask for what we need.

2. Jesus' brief yet persistent prayer teaches us that prayer must be prolonged and steadfast. It's not like turning on a light or flicking a switch. Consider the prayers of St. Monica, for example. Her son, Augustine, was cultured and intelligent, but distant from God. He subscribed to the various philosophical trends that were popular in his day. However, his mother never gave up praying and crying out to God. Years later, when Augustine turned thirty, he converted and became the great saint we know today.

3. Prayer as Jesus teaches us must end by committing ourselves to God's will. We never know what is best for us.

When Jesus returns to the three apostles, he finds them asleep. He turns to Peter, who had just declared his willingness to die for him, and says to him, "So you could not keep watch with me for one hour? Watch and pray that you may not undergo the test. The spirit is willing, but the flesh is weak." What a powerful lesson! The devil always tempts us, and if we're not watchful, we can fall. To avoid falling, we must pray. We are weak, and without God's aid, we cannot withstand trials.

It is apparent that Jesus is seeking support from his companions and is afraid to be by himself. Despite feeling dejected and alone, he prostrates himself on the ground again and prays with the same words. When he checks on his apostles again and finds them asleep once more, he becomes even more distressed. He cries out with "loud cries and tears," as Hebrews tells us (5:7). His anguish is so intense that he sweats blood, and the drops fall to the ground. In this moment of great distress, the Father intervenes and sends an angel to console his Son. Although abandoned by his companions, Jesus is relieved by his Father's care.

Having regained his usual mastery, he hears the crowd of those who have come to arrest him, led by the traitor Judas, and he faces his Passion and death with determination.

12: The Scourging at the Pillar
(THE SECOND SORROWFUL MYSTERY)

Pilate then summoned the chief priests, the rulers, and the people and said to them, "You brought this man to me and accused him of inciting the people to revolt. I have conducted my investigation in your presence and have not found this man guilty of the charges you have brought against him, nor did Herod, for he sent him back to us. So no capital crime has been committed by him. Therefore I shall have him flogged and then release him." (Luke 23:14-16)

Roman scourging was a horrific form of punishment. Cicero, an ancient Roman lawyer, writer, and orator, referred to it as the *horribile flagellum*, meaning the "horrible scourge." The Roman method was different from Jewish scourging, which was limited to forty strokes, and always administered thirty-nine to ensure compliance with the prescription. (St. Paul endured this type of scourging five times.) In contrast, Roman flagellation involved using whips that tore the skin and had no maximum number of blows. The punishment lasted until the condemned person was totally depleted. According to evidence from the Shroud of Turin, Jesus received 120 blows during his scourging.

Pilate's order was promptly carried out, and the soldiers wasted no time in mocking Jesus. They led him into the courtyard, stripped him, and tied his hands behind a low column that was there specifically for this purpose. In this way, his body remained arched and exposed to the blows. The scourgers typically took turns, two at a time, as they struck a condemned man until he was slumped over in agony.

I do not know what Jesus was thinking. Maybe he repeated mentally, "Father, may your will be done." Or perhaps he thought of the verse from Psalms, "I am a worm, not a man" (122:7). He truly saw himself being treated like an object in the hands of those who raged against him, without even knowing him. Sometimes, several days after the flogging, the condemned died from infection or other complications.

When Jesus was forced to stand up, his body must have appeared pitiful, covered in bloody wounds from the scourging. The soldiers had carried out Pilate's order, but they had not yet satisfied their desire to vent their hatred toward the despised Jew. They devised something else to inflict upon him.

13: The Crowning with Thorns
(THE THIRD SORROWFUL MYSTERY)

The soldiers led him away inside the palace, that is, the praetorium, and assembled the whole cohort. They clothed him in purple and, weaving a crown of thorns, placed it on him. They began to salute him with, "Hail, King of the Jews!" and kept striking his head with a reed and spitting upon him. They knelt before him in homage. (Mark 15:16-19)

It appears that the kingship of Jesus went to the heads of Pilate, Herod, and the soldiers. They affixed an inscription in three different languages to the top of the cross, which read, "Jesus of Nazareth, King of the Jews." The soldiers even said to each other, "Let us make him a king our way," and invited all present to take part. From this broad invitation, Jesus knew that he was about to be the centerpiece of a cruel spectacle in which everyone would participate.

It wasn't difficult to make him a king. They chose a scarlet cloth as his cloak, placed a rod in his right hand as a scepter, and used a stool for a throne. The most significant ornament was a crown of thorns, skillfully woven to resemble a royal crown, which they pressed firmly onto Jesus' head. The thorns penetrated his skin, holding the crown in place.

Then the show began. One by one, the soldiers played their parts like actors. In imitation of the greeting addressed to the emperor, they knelt down contemptuously and recited their lines, saying: "Hail, King of the Jews." Then they added to the spectacle. They spat in his face, slapped him, pulled at his beard, and used the rod to strike his head, now crowned with thorns.

The torture and mockery continued until all the soldiers were satisfied. One can only imagine the state Jesus must have been in when he was brought back before Pilate and shown to the people.

Here we must highlight the unforgivable mistake made by Pilate, who was vested with the role of judge. As long as Jesus was alone before him, Pilate could truthfully say, "Do you not know that I have power to release you and I have power to crucify you?" (John 19:10). However, since Pilate had invited the crowd to make their pronouncement, it was no longer within his power to decide what he wanted.

14: The Carrying of the Cross
(THE FOURTH SORROWFUL MYSTERY)

As they led him away they took hold of a certain Simon, a Cyrenian, who was coming in from the country; and after laying the cross on him, they made him carry it behind Jesus. A large crowd of people followed Jesus, including many women who mourned and lamented him. Jesus turned to them and said, "Daughters of Jerusalem, do not weep for me; weep instead for yourselves and for your children, for indeed, the days are coming when people will say, 'Blessed are the barren, the wombs that never bore and the breasts that never nursed.' At that time people will say to the mountains, 'Fall upon us!' and to the hills, 'Cover us!' for if these things are done when the wood is green what will happen when it is dry?" Now two others, both criminals, were led away with him to be executed. (Luke 23:26-32)

Jesus' walk to Calvary was not long, only about 600 meters (2000 ft). However, it was exhausting and humiliating due to his physical condition, considering all that he had been through. The cross consisted of two pieces of wood. The vertical part, called the *stipes* (pole), was tall and thick, and was driven into the ground permanently as a warning to troublemakers. The condemned was forced to carry the wooden crossbeam, the *patibulum*, which was not very heavy in itself, but would have been unbearable for anyone worn out by such mistreatment.

It must have been incredibly humiliating for Jesus to be paraded in front of the crowd in such a condition. His face was disfigured to the point that he was almost unrecognizable. His weakened body, which he dragged along with difficulty, was stooped over by the weight of the wood. Although the Gospel does not mention it, it is possible that he may have fallen during the journey. It also does not say whether his gaze met that of his Mother, who was certainly present on the way to Calvary. Similarly, the Gospel does not mention a woman named Veronica, who, at risk of being chased away by the soldiers, had the courage to go to Jesus and clean his face with her veil. Although these details are not recorded in the Scriptures, they are certainly possible.

The Scriptures do mention that the soldiers were irritated by the slow pace of the pitiful group. As a result, they forced a man returning from the countryside, named Simon of Cyrene, to help carry the wood of Jesus. Simon must have wanted to get out of the way, and he probably initially regretted not having taken a different route into the city. But life is like that sometimes. However, that unexpected episode ensured that Simon of Cyrene would be remembered until the end of times. I also believe that Jesus compensated him, and that he and his family became followers of Jesus. In fact, Mark tells us that Simon was the father of Alexander and Rufus (see 15:21). We do not know anything else about these brothers, other than that they were Christians and well-known within the Jerusalem community.

Among the many insults, especially by the members of the Sanhedrin, there is also a group of pious women who had gone with the Lord from Galilee to Judea. They weep at Jesus' agony. Jesus turns to them and offers a great teaching. It is his last recommendation before dying, yet we often overlook its significance. Jesus teaches something crucial. He says, "Do not weep for me; weep instead for yourselves and for your children... for if these things are done when the wood is green what will happen when it is dry?"

In effect, his last words were these: "If I, who am the green wood, am treated like this and forced to face such a terrible ordeal, what will become of the dry wood? That is, those who die in mortal sin and go to Hell? Hell is a much greater suffering than mine and, above all, is an eternal suffering." We shall soon see that just after being horribly crucified, Jesus was not so much concerned about his own suffering, but primarily with the souls of others.

In this, he tells us that our main daily concern should be to live in God's grace. We are all aware that anyone can die at any age, which is why the Lord admonishes us to always be ready, as we do not know the day or the hour. This should be our daily priority, far more important than any other preoccupation.

15: The Crucifixion

(THE FIFTH SORROWFUL MYSTERY)

Standing by the cross of Jesus were his mother and his mother's sister, Mary the wife of Clopas, and Mary of Magdala. When Jesus saw his mother and the disciple there whom he loved, he said to his mother, "Woman, behold, your son." Then he said to the disciple, "Behold, your mother." And from that hour the disciple took her into his home.

After this, aware that everything was now finished, in order that the scripture might be fulfilled, Jesus said, "I thirst." There was a vessel filled with common wine. So they put a sponge soaked in wine on a sprig of hyssop and put it up to his mouth. When Jesus had taken the wine, he said, "It is finished." And bowing his head, he handed over the spirit. (John 19:25-30)

At this moment, John represents all of us as he "took her into his home"–that is, into his life as a disciple of Jesus who, before the mystery of the cross, embodies the entirety of the radicality that it entails. As disciples, we need certain things, such as the bread of life and participation in divine life, but we also need a Mother like Mary.

In the final act, Jesus gives us one last gift—he proclaims the Motherhood of Mary for each of us. Her Motherhood is very real and aimed at regenerating us in Heaven, directed toward our eternal salvation, and therefore necessary for us. To be reborn in Heaven, we need a Mother.

While reciting this mystery, I usually begin with a reflection before each of the ten Hail Marys, in which I recall the seven phrases proclaimed by Jesus on the cross with prophetic references.

First Hail Mary: "Father, forgive them, they know not what they do" (Luke 23:34). Not only does Jesus forgive, but he also seeks justification. May our forgiveness always be like this.

Second Hail Mary: "Today you will be with me in Paradise" (Luke 23:43). The words of the "good thief" are splendid. He acknowledges his faults, affirms the innocence of Jesus, believes in his royalty, and prays to him, "Remember me when you come into your kingdom" (Luke 23:42). It is not difficult to recognize Jesus when he works miracles. But to recognize him when one is a poor convict dying at his side would take heroic faith.

Third Hail Mary: "Behold, your mother [...] behold, your son." This was not [said] to deprive Mary of her motherhood, but rather to extend it to all of us. Jesus was communicating to his mother the maternal mission she would have for the future. And he was telling us about the necessary aid to which we should resort. Just as Jesus chose the necessity of Mary to become incarnate as a man, he also chose Mary as the necessity for us to be regenerated in Heaven. This is why she follows and helps each of us along our earthly pilgrimage.

Fourth Hail Mary: "My God, my God, why have you forsaken me?" (Mark 15:34). This cry is not one of despair, but arises from feeling extremely beaten down. It is the outpouring of Jesus' humanity, which feels abandoned by God.

Fifth Hail Mary: "I thirst." The torture and significant loss of blood resulted in unbearable thirst. His mouth must have been dry, his tongue stuck to his palate.

Sixth Hail Mary: The prophecy has truly been fulfilled: "For my thirst, they gave me vinegar" (Psalm 69:22). He must have drunk it with avidity and then felt disgust.

Seventh Hail Mary: "They divided his garments by casting lots" (Matthew 27:35). This, too, was done by the soldiers. We note that the only possessions Jesus had left were the clothes he was wearing. With this, his poverty was complete.

Eighth Hail Mary: Now he could say with Job, "Naked I came forth from my mother's womb, and naked shall I go back" (Job 1:21). It should be noted that the Jews considered it repugnant for the crucified to be exposed naked. For this reason, Jewish women offered a cloth to wrap around the waist of the condemned.

Ninth Hail Mary: There was nothing left to say but "It is finished." That is, Jesus had done the will of the Father completely. He had fulfilled all the prophecies about him.

Tenth Hail Mary: "Father, into your hands I commend my spirit" (Luke 23:46). These are the final words of Jesus. He expressed them in a moment of great spiritual aridity, but of total and faithful abandonment. He came into this world sent by the Father, and now he leaves it to return to the Father. Throughout his life, Jesus always expressed his total dependence on the Father–in everything he did and everything he said.

Now, finally, he returns to the one who sent him. At this point, I usually add two mysteries. (I mention this only as an option for those who wish to do the same.)

VI Sorrowful Mystery: The most Sacred Heart of Jesus, pierced by a spear.

VII Sorrowful Mystery: The Immaculate Heart of Mary, pierced by a sword.

THE GLORIOUS MYSTERIES

(Wednesday and Sunday)

16: The Resurrection

(THE FIRST GLORIOUS MYSTERY)

After the sabbath, as the first day of the week was dawning, Mary Magdalene and the other Mary came to see the tomb. And behold, there was a great earthquake; for an angel of the Lord descended from heaven, approached, rolled back the stone, and sat upon it. His appearance was like lightning and his clothing was white as snow. The guards were shaken with fear of him and became like dead men.

Then the angel said to the women in reply, "Do not be afraid! I know that you are seeking Jesus the crucified. He is not here, for he has been raised just as he said. Come and see the place where he lay. Then go quickly and tell his disciples, 'He has been raised from the dead, and he is going before you to Galilee; there you will see him.' Behold, I have told you."

Then they went away quickly from the tomb, fearful yet overjoyed, and ran to announce this to his disciples. And behold, Jesus met them on their way and greeted them. They approached, embraced his feet, and did him homage. Then Jesus said to them, "Do not be afraid. Go tell my

brothers to go to Galilee, and there they will see me."
(Matthew 28:1-10)

When Jesus died, darkness covered the earth. The apostles closed themselves up in houses in Jerusalem, fearful of being arrested as followers of someone who had just been executed. The pious women concerned themselves with going to the tomb to complete the embalming of Jesus.

However, Mary remained serene despite her suffering. She was the only one who was certain that Jesus would fulfill what he had said. No one else was thinking about the Resurrection, and no one else believed in it, despite the many announcements Jesus had made.

The faith of all humanity rests in Mary. She alone held the faith of the nascent Church, which would later be born glorious on the day of Pentecost. This is why in many parts of the Catholic world, during the silence of Holy Saturday (which is defined as an "aliturgic" day; that is, the day when the Holy Sacrifice of the Mass is not celebrated), it is customary to celebrate the "Hour of Mary," a prayer centered on the faith of Mary.

On the third day, Sunday, we celebrate the day of surprises. It is the glorious day of the Resurrection, which no one expected. The primacy of the Resurrection belongs to the pious women, who were closest to Jesus during his Passion, having followed and helped him in his public life. It is fitting that they should be the first witnesses of the Resurrection. All the Gospels agree that the first "witness" of the Resurrection was the empty tomb itself. The first people to see the risen Jesus were the women. Among them, Mary of Magdala holds a special place.

The Gospels do not always agree on the various apparitions of Jesus regarding their sequence and locations. When reading the Gospel, it is important to keep in mind that the evangelists did not intend to write a biography of Jesus. Instead, their goal was to evangelize readers through his teachings. The Gospels are the result of preaching, and they do not focus solely on biographical information. Rather, they gather material freely and aim to remain faithful to the teachings derived from it.

Undoubtedly, the Resurrection of Jesus is the most significant event that validates the entirety of his teachings. Following Easter, Jesus does not reveal himself to everyone, but only to those whom he chose to testify to his Resurrection. He appears to them several times in which he allows them to touch him, eats with them, and imparts his final teachings. However, he does not object to appearing to a larger audience. In fact, St. Paul recounts an apparition of the Risen One to a crowd of some 500 people. His primary focus is to prepare future preachers.

It might be surprising to learn that the apostles had difficulty recognizing Jesus after his Resurrection. This was primarily due to their shock at seeing him alive again, having been certain of his death and burial. Initially, they mistook him for a ghost. This is why he allowed them to touch him and even ate with them—to dispel their doubts.

There was probably also a difference in his appearance before and after his death. The Gospels tell us that Jesus did not reveal himself in his glorified body—as he is in Heaven and as he appeared during the Transfiguration. In any case, the body of the Risen One, which was no longer subject to suffering, must have already had a celestial appearance that made him appear different from before. Jesus' words help them greatly to recognize him.

Taking into account Jesus' words to the women, whom he asked to tell his "brothers" (note the affectionate term) to go to Galilee, I am inclined to think that Jesus first appeared to the women that Sunday, then to Peter, and afterwards to the two disciples from Emmaus. I believe that most of the other apparitions occurred in Galilee. The appearance to Thomas, the apostle who doubted unless he could see and touch for himself (see John 20:25), is noteworthy. Then there is the apparition in which Jesus bestowed upon the apostles the power to forgive sins. Lastly, I believe he invited the apostles to return to Jerusalem for further instruction and to witness his Ascension into Heaven.

17: The Ascension

(THE SECOND GLORIOUS MYSTERY)

While they were still speaking about this, he stood in their midst and said to them, "Peace be with you." But they were startled and terrified and thought that they were seeing a ghost. Then he said to them, "Why are you troubled? And why do questions arise in your hearts? Look at my hands and my feet, that it is I myself. Touch me and see, because a ghost does not have flesh and bones as you can see I have." And as he said this, he showed them his hands and his feet. While they were still incredulous for joy and were amazed, he asked them, "Have you anything here to eat?" They gave him a piece of baked fish; he took it and ate it in front of them.

He said to them, "These are my words that I spoke to you while I was still with you, that everything written about me in the law of Moses and in the prophets and psalms must be fulfilled." Then he opened their minds to understand the scriptures. And he said to them, "Thus it is written that the Messiah would suffer and rise from the dead on the third day and that repentance, for the forgiveness of sins, would be preached in his name to all the nations, beginning from Jerusalem. You are witnesses of these things. And [behold]

I am sending the promise of my Father upon you; but stay in the city until you are clothed with power from on high."

Then he led them [out] as far as Bethany, raised his hands, and blessed them. As he blessed them he parted from them and was taken up to heaven. (Luke 24:36-51)

This is the final act of Jesus' earthly life. After the forty days in which he showed himself alive, he says that having come from the Father, he now returns to the Father. His final recommendations are very important. First of all, he promises to send the Holy Spirit, who will remain permanently with them. He will strengthen them and help them recall and remember vividly all the words that Jesus said to them. In addition, he will add many things that Jesus did not say, because the disciples were not yet ready to receive them.

Jesus recommends they stay in Jerusalem until they are empowered from above (that is, by the Holy Spirit). Then they must go and preach in Jerusalem, in Samaria, and to the ends of the earth. Finally, he reassures them, "And behold, I am with you always, until the end of the age" (Matthew 28:20).

These promises fill the disciples with joy, despite the sadness of separation. After blessing them, Jesus ascends to Heaven. The apostles do not take their eyes off him until a cloud hides him from their sight.

18: The Descent of the Holy Spirit

(THE THIRD GLORIOUS MYSTERY)

When the time for Pentecost was fulfilled, they were all in one place together. And suddenly there came from the sky a noise like a strong driving wind, and it filled the entire house in which they were. Then there appeared to them tongues as of fire, which parted and came to rest on each one of them. And they were all filled with the holy Spirit and began to speak in different tongues, as the Spirit enabled them to proclaim.

Now there were devout Jews from every nation under heaven staying in Jerusalem. At this sound, they gathered in a large crowd, but they were confused because each one heard them speaking in his own language. (Acts 2:1-6)

The descent of the Holy Spirit is preceded by nine days of intense prayer, with Mary and others. The disciples pray in the temple or in the great hall of the last supper. Perhaps it was also a period of intimacy. Who knows how many questions they asked Mary about the birth and childhood of Jesus?

The solemn descent of the Holy Spirit takes place on the morning of the day of Pentecost. It is preceded by a strong wind, so much so that it shakes the house with a noise so great that it is heard in a large part of the city, and people rush to see what has happened. The apostles are not at all frightened. They see tongues of fire coming down and resting on each one present. Immediately, they feel strength and courage. They begin to speak different languages as the Spirit prompts them.

The pious Israelites had gathered in Jerusalem from all over the region to celebrate the feast of Pentecost; that is Shavuot. As many people were arriving, the apostles hurried among them to bear witness to the Resurrection of Jesus. Then, they experience another surprise: the gift of tongues is multiplied. The apostles are amazed to discover that the people understand them despite the different languages. The people, too, are astonished by this: everyone understands them and hears them speaking in their own language. The apostles now realize that their mission is open before them; they will be understood everywhere.

The apostles realize that Peter is about to address the enormous crowd. Perhaps the other ten apostles stand in formation behind him, providing their testimony to affirm his words. This initial discourse by St. Peter proves to be highly fruitful, resulting in 3,000 people being persuaded and requesting baptism. I believe it was at this moment when Peter truly grasped the significance of Jesus' words: "Come after me, and I will make you fishers of men" (Matthew 4:19). Previously, he marveled at the miraculous catch of 153 large fish (see John 21:11). Now, he recognizes the tremendous impact of convincing 3,000 individuals with just one sermon.

On that Pentecost day, with the descent of the Holy Spirit, the Church was born. The Spirit would never abandon the great work of salvation founded by Jesus Christ.

19: The Assumption

(THE FOURTH GLORIOUS MYSTERY)

And Mary said: "My soul proclaims the greatness of the Lord; my spirit rejoices in God my savior. For he has looked upon his handmaid's lowliness; behold, from now on will all ages call me blessed. The Mighty One has done great things for me, and holy is his name. His mercy is from age to age to those who fear him." (Luke 1:46-50)

Now we arrive at the glorification of Mary, whom Dante defines as "more humble and sublime than any creature" (*Paradiso*, XXXIII, 2). Immediately after being called "Mother of God" for the first time by Elizabeth, Mary bursts into a song in which she reflects on herself: "The Lord has turned his gaze on my humility and made great things in me, and holy is his name." From this magnificent portrait that Mary presents at the beginning of her calling as Mother of God, we can contemplate the earthly culmination of Our Lady, when she was assumed body and soul into Heaven.

Pope Pius XII pronounced the dogma of the Assumption with the words: "The Immaculate Mother of God, the ever Virgin Mary, having completed the course of her earthly life, was assumed body and soul into heavenly glory" (Apostolic Constitution, *Munificentissimus Deus*, 44, November 1, 1950). The pope does not delve into the question of whether she died. This is an issue of personal value and does not affect matters of faith. After all, death is a universal human experience; for, even Jesus died. Therefore, there is no reason to assume that Mary, who lived a humble life, would have been exempt from death. Furthermore, the liturgical feast of the "Dormition of Mary," which has been celebrated for centuries in the Eastern Church alongside the Assumption, should not be silenced.

The Assumption of Mary is a profoundly significant event in the plan of salvation and it has immense salvific implications. Mary's role in the Incarnation of Jesus, as divinely ordained, was irreplaceable. However, Mary's mission does not conclude with her death. While her earthly mission pertaining to Christ required a humble and suffering body, her mission toward us, which persists until the end of time, necessitates a spiritual and glorious body, always intertwined with Christ. Scripture consistently attests to the unbreakable bond between Jesus and Mary during their earthly lives, making it logical to expect this bond to persist in their heavenly existence.

Christ's earthly existence was marked by the constraints of a mortal body, characterized by suffering and limitations. However, through his Resurrection, he experiences a new birth, obtaining a spiritual body free from human limitations and imbued with a glory and strength he did not possess before. This is the living and risen Jesus whom the apostles promptly proclaim to the masses and who is present in the Eucharist. Moreover, this transformation that Jesus demonstrates for himself and for us is a direct consequence of his Resurrection. It is not merely a simple transition from earth to Heaven, but a profound metamorphosis and glorification of the entire human being, encompassing both soul and body.

In relation to Mary, as she was chosen for her mission to the Son, just as the fruits of Jesus' Passion were anticipated to her, enabling her to be conceived without original sin, likewise, in anticipation of her current mission, the glorification of her body was granted. This is the essence of the Assumption: Mary participates in the complete glorification of her Son, being united with him in the work of universal mediation with the Father. As a result, she remains alive and present among us, adorned with the glory to which we are all called, and we look to her as the fulfillment of our hope.

Assumed into Heaven, Mary was immediately enveloped in the boundless love of the Father, the Son, and the Holy Spirit. She gazed upon the Most Holy Trinity, as one, in her contemplation: one God in three persons. This awe-inspiring vision bestowed upon her infinite joy, and she knew that this vision and joy would accompany her throughout eternity.

This abundance of divine grace is the promise that God holds for each one of us if we wholeheartedly love him with all our mind, heart, and strength. How can we attain it? Jesus has shown us the path: by striving to love him and our neighbor as he has loved us.

Here, when we view life through the lens of faith, we come to understand that the Glorious Mysteries are interconnected with the preceding three. As we wholeheartedly embrace and live the Joyful Mysteries (with Jesus' continuous presence in the Eucharist), the Luminous Mysteries (with the teachings of Jesus in the Gospel), and the Sorrowful Mysteries (through our participation in the suffering of Jesus), we are better prepared to fully experience and live the Glorious Mysteries. We can say well, as in the quote [attributed to St. Francis of Assisi]: "So great is the good which I expect that all pain is to me a delight."

20: The Coronation of Our Lady

(THE FIFTH GLORIOUS MYSTERY)

A great sign appeared in the sky, a woman clothed with the sun, with the moon under her feet, and on her head a crown of twelve stars. She was with child and wailed aloud in pain as she labored to give birth.

Then another sign appeared in the sky; it was a huge red dragon, with seven heads and ten horns, and on its heads were seven diadems. Its tail swept away a third of the stars in the sky and hurled them down to the earth. Then the dragon stood before the woman about to give birth, to devour her child when she gave birth. She gave birth to a son, a male child, destined to rule all the nations with an iron rod. Her child was caught up to God and his throne. (Revelation 12:1-5)

Here, we are presented with a great sign, one that echoes a significant event from the past. In the early stages of human history, soon after the transgression of our ancestors Adam and Eve, God prophesied the coming of a woman who would be marked by an unyielding enmity toward Satan, who had cunningly appeared in the form of a serpent. Furthermore, God revealed that this woman's Son would triumphantly crush the head of the serpent. (See Genesis 3:15.)

We have now reached the culmination of human history. The remarkable sign before us remains a magnificent woman, now adorned with a crown as the Queen. She continues her valiant struggle against Satan, who appears in the form of a menacing red dragon. The Son of this woman is none other than Jesus, who reigns over all nations with an unyielding authority. It is through this very authority that he triumphs over Satan, wielding an iron scepter as the instrument of victory.

It is indeed true that biblical scholars interpret various profiles represented by this woman, highlighting the diverse figures often used to symbolize the same person in the Bible. However, it is evident to me that Mary is the central figure being portrayed, considering that she is the one who gives birth to Jesus, the child in question.

Assumed into Heaven, Mary finds eternal joy in continuously beholding her son, as if it were the first time. She sees him in the fullness of what she had always believed him to be: fully human and fully divine. However, there is a significant difference between believing and actually seeing. Mary now witnesses Jesus in his definitive and everlasting glory, recognizing him as the King of Heaven and Earth, leading all of creation and the great human family that he has redeemed through his Passion and death. She grasps the profound fulfillment of the prophecy that Gabriel shared with her on the day of the Annunciation. "You will conceive in your womb and bear a son, and you shall name him Jesus. He will be great and will be called Son of the Most High, and the Lord God will give him the throne of David his father, and he will rule over the house of Jacob forever, and of his kingdom there will be no end" (Luke 1:31-33). Finally, the Kingdom of God is fulfilled.

In the vast Kingdom over which Christ reigns as King, Mary is exalted to the position of Queen, alongside Jesus himself, who has crowned her as Queen of Heaven and Earth. This is Mary's glorious and everlasting place.

It is truly beneficial for us to call upon her intercession, for she loves each of us individually, as if we were the only ones in existence. Today, I encourage you to invoke her as the "Queen of Peace," as she introduced herself in Medjugorje, understanding the pressing need for peace in our world. Let us also invoke her as the "Queen of Families," recognizing the brokenness that afflicts many families today. And let us not forget the various titles with which she is invoked as "Queen" in the Litany of Loreto, embracing her multifaceted role and seeking her powerful intercession.

To better understand the greatness of what God has created, let us think of how wondrously he has redeemed [the world]. The triune God, through the Word and for Jesus, brought forth the universe into existence. It is vital for us to constantly remember that Jesus Christ is the ultimate purpose and meaning of our existence. Let us embrace the profound truth and declare, "Jesus, I was born through you, and you are the very reason for my being."

This purpose gives us an unparalleled and uplifting goal: to be united with him in Heaven. As history unfolded, we witnessed the fall of our first parents and the subsequent redemption brought forth by Jesus himself. At the end of time, there will be the resurrection of the body and the final judgment. For the faithful, God will be all in all, encompassing every aspect of our lives. Such is the extraordinary destiny that awaits us.

Thus, we come to comprehend the immense power of Mary Most Holy. As the Queen of Heaven and Earth, she reigns over us, guided by her Immaculate Heart, which overflows with boundless love. Though she is reliant on Jesus, she governs us with a strength that knows no limits.

APPENDICES

Appendix I: The Popes of the Rosary

Pope St. Pius V (Antonio Ghislieri) can truly be called "the first pope of the rosary." His papal bull *Consueverunt Romani Pontifices* (September 17, 1569) is considered the "Magna Carta" of the rosary. Whoever prays the rosary should be familiar with it. In this bull, the Church put forth for the first time a classic definition of the rosary. That definition, later modified, would enter the Dominican breviary and later the Roman one.

St. Pius V wrote:

> Prompted by their example, and, as is piously believed, by the Holy Ghost, the inspired Blessed founder of the Order of Friars Preachers, (whose institutes and rule we ourselves expressly professed when we were in minor orders), in circumstances similar to those in which we now find ourselves, when parts of France and of Italy were unhappily troubled by the heresy of the Albigensians, which blinded so many of the worldly that they were raging most savagely against the priests of the Lord and the clergy, raised his eyes up unto Heaven, unto that mountain of the Glorious Virgin Mary, loving Mother of God. For she by her seed has crushed the head of the twisted serpent, and has alone destroyed all heresies, and by the blessed fruit of her womb has saved a world condemned by the fall of our first parent. From her, without human hand, was that stone cut, which, struck by wood, poured forth the abundantly flowing waters of graces. And so Dominic looked to that simple way of praying and beseeching God, accessible to all and wholly pious, which is called the Rosary, or Psalter of the Blessed Virgin Mary, in which the same most

Blessed Virgin is venerated by the angelic greeting repeated one hundred and fifty times, that is, according to the number of the Davidic Psalter, and by the Lord's Prayer with each decade. Interposed with these prayers are certain meditations showing forth the entire life of Our Lord Jesus Christ, thus completing the method of prayer devised by the by the Fathers of the Holy Roman Church. This same method St. Dominic propagated, and it was, spread by the Friars of Blessed Dominic, namely, of the aforementioned Order, and accepted by not a few of the people. Christ's faithful, inflamed by these prayers, began immediately to be changed into new men. The darkness of heresy began to be dispelled, and the light of the Catholic Faith to be revealed. Sodalities for this form of prayer began to be instituted in many places by the Friars of the same Order, legitimately deputed to this work by their Superiors, and confreres began to be enrolled together.

Here we witness the fervent support of St. Pius V for devotion to the rosary. Another significant confirmation of his devotion is the historical event that took place on October 7, 1571. St. Pius V declared that the Battle of Lepanto, which was fought against the Turks, was won through the intercession of Our Lady of the Rosary. In recognition of this miraculous victory, he proclaimed that day as the feast of Our Lady of the Rosary.

Then there was Blessed Pius IX (Giovanni Maria Mastai Ferretti). A few days after the opening of the First Vatican Council, Pope Pius penned his apostolic letter *Egregiis suis*. He wrote:

How St. Dominic used this prayer (the rosary) as an invincible weapon to disperse the nefarious Albigensian heresy, which threatened the peace and tranquility of the Christian society, so the faithful, educated and clothed with this singular type of armor, that is, of the daily recitation of the rosary of the Blessed Virgin Mary, will achieve more easily the intent to annihilate so many monstrous errors everywhere arising, with the powerful aid of the Immaculate Mother of God and with the authority of the Ecumenical Vatican Council convened by us, and to be inaugurated soon.

The council was opened on December 8 of that year.

After Pius IX, there was Leo XIII. He, too, can be called a "pope of the rosary" on par with Pope Pius V. He wrote no fewer than twelve encyclical letters and two apostolic letters in which he expounded important teaching regarding the rosary. During his long papacy (1878-1903), the practice of consecrating the month of October to the rosary was begun. He referred to the rosary as "a distinctive honorific of Christian piety," "the most welcome of prayers," and "the tile of our faith and the compendium of devotion owed to (the Virgin)."

Pope Leo XIII saw in the rosary "a simple way to make the main dogmas of the Christian faith penetrate and inculcate in souls." In addressing the societal challenges of his time, Pope Leo XIII, who authored the influential encyclical *Rerum Novarum*, encouraged and urged the faithful to embrace the rosary. He recognized that by placing one's faith in and gazing on the sufferings of Christ, one could overcome aversion to sacrifice and suffering. Similarly, contemplating the humility of the Savior and Mary could help Christians overcome their aversion to leading a humbling and industrial life. Moreover, meditating on the mysteries of the glory of Christ, Mary, and the saints could restore a sense of value to the mysteries of the future life and alleviate attachment to material possessions. Pope Leo XIII passionately praised and encouraged the rosary. In fact, at least twenty-two documents, both major and minor, have been counted in this regard.

St. Pius X, born Giuseppe Sarto, wrote numerous Marian documents in which he frequently recommended the recitation of the rosary. However, none of his encyclicals were dedicated [exclusively] to the rosary, since his predecessor Pope Leo XIII had already done so much in this respect. In a letter written to Fr. Costanzo Becchi, a Dominican who in 1900 had reestablished the Association of the Perpetual Rosary in Florence, Pope Pius X said that the rosary "constitutes prayer par excellence." In his testament, he recommended the rosary as "the prayer that is the most beautiful of all, the richest in graces, and the one that pleases the Most Holy Virgin."

Pope Benedict XV (Giacomo Della Chiesa) wrote of the rosary in his encyclical *Fausto Appetente Die* (1921), which he released on the occasion of the seventh centenary of the death of St. Dominic who, according to tradition and as already mentioned, was the instrument by which "Mary used her holy rosary to teach the Church." He defined the rosary as a "gentle prayer... both vocal and mental." In a signed letter, he wrote: "The Christian people (...) should hold firmly that (the rosary) is the most beautiful flower of human piety and the most fruitful source of heavenly graces." Finally, he highlighted it as "the universal character of collective and domestic prayer."

Moving on to more recent times, Pope Pius XII wrote one encyclical and eight letters on the rosary, and gave many discourses. He referred to the rosary as "a synthesis of the entire Gospel, a meditation on the mysteries of the Lord, an evening sacrifice, a crown of roses, a hymn of praise, a family prayer, a compendium of Christian life, a sure pledge of heavenly favor, and a safeguard for salvation."

In his papal encyclical, *Ingruentium Malorum* (1951), he wrote:

> By no means is there only one way to pray to obtain this aid. However, We consider the Holy Rosary the most convenient and most fruitful means, as is clearly suggested by the very origin of this practice, heavenly rather than human, and by its nature. (...) We do not hesitate to affirm again publicly that We put great confidence in the Holy Rosary for the healing of evils which afflict our times. Not with force, not with arms,

not with human power, but with Divine help obtained through the means of this prayer, strong like David with his sling, the Church undaunted shall be able to confront the infernal enemy.

Pope St. John XXIII honored the rosary as pope, as well as throughout his life. He referred to it as an essential component of his spirituality, according to what he revealed in *Journal of the Soul*. He explained his teaching on the rosary several times in encyclicals and speeches. Among the first, we recall *Grata Recordatio* (1959), in which he recommended the devotion of the month of October. He also recalled the magisterium of his predecessors, especially Leo XIII. And he added to the beautiful definition of Pope Pius V:

> For the rosary is a very commendable form of prayer and meditation. In saying it we weave a mystic garland of *Ave Marias*, *Pater Nosters*, and *Gloria Patris*. And as we recite these vocal prayers, we meditate upon the principal mysteries of our religion; the Incarnation of Jesus Christ and the Redemption of the human race are proposed, one event after another, for our consideration.

Pope John XXIII also wrote an apostolic letter, *Il Religioso Convegno* (1961), a touching and paternal treatise for the faithful. In fresh language, he communicated the value and efficacy of the rosary in what can be considered a veritable *summa* of the rosary itself.

After John XXIII, Pope Paul VI (Giovanni Battista Montini) was elected to the throne of Peter. In his encyclical *Christi Matri* he wrote:

> The Second Vatican Council recommended use of the Rosary to all the sons of the Church, not in express words but in unmistakable fashion in this phrase: "Let them value highly the pious practices and exercises directed to the Blessed Virgin and approved over the centuries by the magisterium.

Paul VI reiterated the same recommendation to be friends of the rosary in the Year of Prayer to Mary (1972) and particularly in *Marialis Cultus* (1974), in which he affirmed that the rosary is a very noble and integral part of Christian worship. In *Marialis Cultus*, he recalled the Dominicans: "Among these people special mention should be made of the sons of St. Dominic, by tradition the guardians and promoters of this very salutary practice."

I would like to pause for a moment on Albino Luciani, who after serving as patriarch of Venice became Pope John Paul I (August 26-September 28, 1978). He was a born catechist, and as a catechist, he had all the qualities of simplicity, vivaciousness, liveliness, and persuasive exemplifications. What did he think of the rosary? [As cardinal] on October 7, 1973, in a homily held in the Jesuit church, on the occasion of the fourth centenary of the Feast of the Rosary, responding to various objections to the rosary, he expressed himself in this way:

> Some people criticize the rosary. They say it is a childish prayer, superstitious, not good enough for adult Christians. Or that it is an automatic prayer, a monotonous and boring repetition of the Hail Mary. Or again: it is not for our day, today we can do better: read the Bible, for example, which compared to the rosary is like good flour compared to bran!

> Allow me to offer you a couple of impressions on this matter as a pastor of souls.

> First impression: The crisis of the rosary will occur later. In our day, it is preceded by a general crisis in prayer. People are totally absorbed in their material interests; they hardly ever think of their soul, noise has invaded our life. Macbeth could say once again: "I have killed sleep, I have killed silence!" It is difficult for us to find a brief moment for our spiritual life, for a "*dulcis*

91

sermocinatio" (sweet conversation) with God. This is a great pity. Donoso Cortes used to say: "Our world today is in a poor state because there are more battles than there are prayers." Community liturgies are celebrated. This is very good but not sufficient: personal conversation with God is also necessary.

Second impression. When we refer to "adult Christians" in the context of prayer, we sometimes exaggerate. Personally, when I engage in intimate conversation with God or the Blessed Virgin Mary, I prefer to see myself as a child rather than an adult. The trappings of authority, such as the miter, skullcap, and ring, fade away. I give myself permission to set aside the weighty responsibilities and serious contemplations that come with adulthood and the role of a bishop. Instead, I allow myself to embrace the spontaneous tenderness of a child in the presence of their father or mother. For at least half an hour, I can be before God as my true self, acknowledging my weaknesses and also the best parts of me. I feel the inner child of yesteryears resurface, longing to engage in conversation, to share and express love for the Lord, and sometimes even to cry out for mercy. All of this aids me in prayer. The rosary, a simple and accessible prayer, allows me to reconnect with the innocence and vulnerability of childhood, and I am not ashamed to admit it.

The rosary a prayer of repetition? Père de Foucauld used to say: "Love is expressed in a few words, always the same, repeated over and over again."

Is the Bible important? Absolutely, it is the ultimate source. However, not everyone has the expertise or time to read it extensively. For those who do read it, there are moments when it can be helpful to turn to Our Lady, seeing her as a mother and sister, especially during travel or in times of specific need. While reading the Bible is valuable as a scholarly pursuit, meditating on and savoring the mysteries of the rosary can provide a profound spiritual understanding, like extracting the essence from the Bible.

Is the rosary a sentimental prayer? It depends. Instead, it can be a prayer filled with joy and gladness. When practiced correctly, the rosary becomes a contemplation focused on Mary, intensifying as one progresses. It can also become a heartfelt refrain that, when repeated, brings a sweet and melodic solace to the soul.

Is the rosary a poor prayer? And what, then, will rich prayer be? The rosary is a parade of *Paters*, prayers taught by Jesus; of *Aves*, God's greeting to the Virgin through the angel; of *Glorias*, praise to the Most Holy Trinity. Or would you like–instead–the high theological elucubrations? They would not suit the poor, the old, the humble, the simple. The rosary expresses faith without false problems, without subterfuges and mincing words. It aids in abandonment to God, the generous acceptance of suffering. God also makes use of theologians, but to distribute his graces, he makes use above all of the lowliness of the humble and of those who abandon themselves to his will.

As for the relationship between the rosary and the Bible, he replied simply: "After all, the rosary is all Bible: the mysteries are meditations on the Gospel, the Hail Mary and the Our Father are Gospel."

Luciani was so devoted to the rosary, he offered an overall look at the content of the rosary, that is, at the mysteries contemplated in it. Speaking in Pompeii, on the centenary of the image of the Our Lady of the Rosary, on October 1, 1975, he said:

> (Glorious Mysteries): Christ is not risen solitarily (…) immediately after him comes Our Lady.
>
> (Sorrowful Mysteries): We are (…) co-heirs with Christ, if we truly share in the sufferings of Christ we also share in his glory (see Rom 8:17). This is why in the rosary we also contemplate Mary's suffering (…) in certain moments, her trials became acute.
>
> (Joyful Mysteries): Fortunately, life–with its suffering– also knows joys; we remember those of Mary in the Joyful Mysteries. In the Annunciation, the joy was not only of feeling chosen by God, but of assuming with deliberate responsibility a very great mission…
>
> The birth of Jesus with the various circumstances brings her an inexpressible joy…

Some ask about the five beads at the top of the rosary, above the small crucifix. What are they? Are they an ornament? Patriarch Luciani gave a satisfactory answer to this question. Speaking to the Canossian Sisters of Sant'Alvisein about prayer (1976), he said:

> It is not a question of adding new prayers, but rather of using the common ones. Few, for example, use the first beads of the crown in the holy rosary. Some–and this is completely free–recite the Creed on the first bead intending to stand firm in the truths revealed by God. The following three beads indicate three Hail Marys to preserve the three fundamental virtues: 1) Hail Mary, so that my faith may increase; 2) Hail Mary, so that I may grow in the flame of my love; 3) Hail Mary, so that my hope may become stronger. The last bead, before the decade is a Glory to the Most Holy Trinity.

I believe that everyone knows of the tender and constant devotion of Pope St. John Paul II to the rosary. It was his favorite prayer. In his encyclical *Rosarium Virginis Mariae*, he completed the rosary by adding the optional Luminous Mysteries. Here is a passage from the encyclical that concerns the Dominicans:

> The history of the Rosary shows how this prayer was used in particular by the Dominicans at a difficult time for the Church due to the spread of heresy. Today we are facing new challenges. Why should we not once more have recourse to the Rosary, with the same faith as those who have gone before us? The Rosary retains all its power and continues to be a valuable pastoral resource for every good evangelizer.

According to Pope St. John Paul II, the rosary is the contemplation of the face of Christ in the company and at the school of his Most Holy Mother. Reciting the rosary is nothing other than contemplating the face of Christ with Mary.

Pope Benedict XVI, too, spoke about the rosary on various occasions. Listed here are some of his statements (which can also be used as daily meditations):

> The sacred rosary is not a mere relic of the past, nor should it be regarded as an antiquated prayer evoking nostalgia. On the contrary, the rosary is currently undergoing a renewed blossoming. This resurgence serves as a powerful testament to the love that younger generations hold for Jesus and his blessed Mother, Mary.
>
> In today's dispersive world, this prayer helps to place Christ at the center, as did the Virgin, who meditated inwardly on everything that was said about her Son, and then what he did and said.

When reciting the rosary, the important and meaningful moments of salvation history are relived. The various steps of Christ's mission are traced.

With Mary, the heart is oriented toward the mystery of Jesus. We put Christ at the center of our life, of our time, of our cities, through the contemplation and meditation of his holy mysteries of joy, light, sorrow, and glory.

May Mary help us to welcome the grace that emanates from these mysteries, so that through us she can "irrigate" society, starting with our daily relationships, and purify it from the many negative forces by opening it to the newness of God.

When prayed authentically, not mechanically and superficially, but with depth and sincerity, the rosary brings peace and reconciliation. It holds within it the healing power of the Most Holy Name of Jesus, invoked with faith and love at the center of each "Hail Mary."

When the rosary is not reduced to mechanical repetition of traditional formulas, it becomes a profound biblical meditation that immerses us in the events of the Lord's life, accompanied by the Blessed Virgin Mary, who, like us, preserved them in her heart.

As the month of May comes to an end, let us not abandon this practice, but rather let us continue it with even greater commitment. May the lessons learned during this month continue to illuminate the lamp of faith in the hearts of Christians and in their homes.

> [In the recitation of the holy rosary,] I entrust to you the most urgent intentions of my ministry, the needs of the Church, the grave problems of humanity: peace in the world, unity among Christians, dialogue between all cultures.

Finally, we arrive at Pope Francis. In my opinion, the most significant words he has said thus far about the rosary are recorded in a handwritten preface to a book on Marian prayer. In the Italian edition of the book, *Il Rosario. Preghiera del cuore* ("The Rosary, Prayer of the heart"), written by his secretary and priest of the Catholic Coptic rite Fr. Yoannis Lahzi Gaid, he wrote: "The rosary is a prayer that always accompanies me; it is also the prayer of ordinary people and the saints… it is a prayer from my heart." These words were dated (with significance) May 13, 2014, the feast of Our Lady of Fatima.

Francis' opening remarks are consistent with his well-known gestures and speeches. His regular visits to the Marian icon Salus Populi Romani, which is revered in the Basilica of Santa Maria Maggiore, have become a familiar routine. (Pope Francis prays there before every international trip and upon return.) He also has a deep devotion to Our Lady Undoer of Knots, an image of German origin that he brought to Argentina.

Regarding the rosary, in March [2014], Monsignor Alfred Xuereb while speaking with Radio Vaticana, recalled the first year of Pope Francis' pontificate. Referring to Francis, he said:

> He has not wasted a minute! He works tirelessly and, when he feels the need to take a moment's pause, he closes his eyes and does nothing: he simply sits and prays the Rosary. I think he prays at least three rosaries. And he told me: "This helps me to relax." Then he goes back to work.

Appendix II: A History of the Rosary

The origin of the rosary dates back to the monasteries. In ancient times, the monks used to recite all 150 Psalms of David. However, it was challenging for both the monks and the faithful who attended the liturgies to memorize all the Psalms. Around the year 850, an Irish monk suggested substituting the recitation of the Psalms with 150 Our Fathers. This proposal gained acceptance, and the faithful, as well as the monks, began to count their prayers in various ways. Some used pebbles, others employed strings, and some even prayed with knots. Over the years, these knots and pebbles evolved into what we know as the rosary.

Its name was conceived in the twelfth century by the Cistercian monks. They referred to it as the rosary because they likened it to a crown of mystical roses offered to the Blessed Virgin Mary. Soon after, St. Dominic popularized the rosary. Moreover, he recognized its potential as a powerful tool for Christians to combat heresies.

However, the Mysteries as we know them today were not yet fully developed at that time. It was in the thirteenth century that theologians, inspired by the study of the 150 Psalms, began to see them as veiled prophecies about the life of Jesus. This exploration of the Psalms eventually led to the formulation of psalters focused on Jesus and dedicated to Mary. As a result, four distinct psalters were developed: one consisting of 150 Our Fathers, another with 150 angelic greetings, a third containing 150 praises of Jesus, and a fourth with 150 praises of Mary.

Around the year 1350, the Hail Mary prayer took shape as we know it today. Its development can be attributed to the Carthusian monks who combined the angel Gabriel's greeting

("Hail Mary, full of Grace...") with Elizabeth's words ("Blessed art thou among women...") and added "... now and at the hour of our death. Amen."

In the fourteenth century, particularly among the Cistercians in the region of Trèves (now Trier) in France, additional clauses were inserted after the name of Jesus to encompass the life of Christ within the prayer. During the mid-fourteenth century, a monk named Henry of Kalkar from the Carthusian monastery in Cologne introduced the practice of reciting one Our Father before each decade. This method quickly gained popularity and spread throughout Europe.

Still in the Carthusian monastery of Trèves, at the beginning of the 1400s, Dominic Hélion–also known as Dominic the Prussian or Dominic of Trèves–developed a rosary, in which he succeeded the name of Jesus with fifty passages that retraced his life. Similar to what Henry of Kalkar introduced, Dominic the Prussian's thoughts were divided into groups of ten with an Our Father at the beginning of each group.

Between 1435 and 1445, Dominic composed 150 passages for the Flemish Carthusian lay brothers who recited the Psalter of Mary. These passages were divided into three sections corresponding to the Gospels of Christ's infancy, his public life, and the Passion-Resurrection.

In 1470, the Dominican Alan de la Roche, who had learned how to recite the rosary from the Carthusians, established the first Confraternity of the Rosary. This led to a rapid dissemination of this form of prayer. He referred to the rosary with a reflection attached to each Hail Mary as the "new rosary," while the one consisting solely of Hail Marys without meditations was called the "old rosary."

In addition to Alan de la Roche, another Dominican, St. Peter of Verona, also spread the Marian confraternities far and wide. Alan de la Roche reduced the mysteries to fifteen and subdivided them into three: Joyful, Sorrowful, and Glorious. As we have said, it was Pope St. John Paul II (a great apostle of the rosary), who in his apostolic letter *Rosarium Virginis Mariae* (2002), introduced the Luminous Mysteries focusing on the public life of Jesus.

Thus, the Dominicans played a significant role in promoting the rosary worldwide. They established several rosary associations, including the "Confraternity of the Most Holy Rosary" founded in 1470. Another notable association is the "Confraternity of the Perpetual Rosary," also known as the "Guard of Honor," which was founded in 1630 by Father Timothy de Ricci. This association committed to reciting the rosary every hour of the day and night, throughout the entire year. Additionally, the Dominican tertiary Pauline-Marie Jaricot founded the "Association of the Living Rosary" in 1826. The medieval structure of the rosary was abandoned gradually with the Renaissance, but the definitive form of the rosary came about in 1521 by the Dominican Albert of Castello.

St. Pius V, who trained under the Dominicans, is known as the first "pope of the rosary." In 1569, he described the great fruits reaped by St. Dominic in the prayer, and he invited all Christians to pray it. Pope Leo XIII, with his twelve encyclicals dedicated to the rosary, is considered the second "Pope of the rosary." From 1478 to today, there have been more than 200 pontifical documents written on the rosary.

In several apparitions, Our Lady herself has revealed the rosary as the most necessary prayer for the good of humanity. During her apparition in Lourdes in 1858, the Virgin Mary appeared with a long rosary on her arm. Similarly, in Fatima in 1917, and more recently in Medjugorje, Our Lady has invited and continues to exhort the faithful to recite the rosary daily.

How to Pray the Rosary

1. Make the Sign of the Cross and say: "O God, come to my assistance. Lord, make haste to help me."
2. Next, say the *Apostles' Creed*.
3. On the first bead, say one *Our Father*.
4. Say one *Hail Mary* on each of the next three beads.
5. Say the *Glory Be*.
6. Then, for each of the five decades, announce the Mystery. (For example, in the first Mystery of Joy, we contemplate the Annunciation.)
7. Say one *Our Father*.
8. Then, for each of the ten beads of the decade, say a *Hail Mary*, while meditating on the Mystery.
9. At the conclusion, say a *Glory Be*.
10. After finishing each decade, you can say the following prayer requested by the Blessed Virgin Mary at Fatima: *O my Jesus, forgive us our sins, save us from the fires of Hell; lead all souls to Heaven, especially those who have most need of thy mercy.*
11. After saying the five decades, conclude with the *Hail, Holy Queen*, followed by this dialogue and prayer:
    V. Pray for us, O holy Mother of God.
    R. That we may be made worthy of the promises of Christ.

About the Author

Father Gabriele Amorth (1925-2016) was a priest of the Congregation of St. Paul. He is considered the most famous Catholic exorcist of the modern era. By his account, he performed at least 60,000 exorcisms during the course of his ministry, sparking a renewed interest in exorcism. In 1994, he co-founded the International Association of Exorcists; almost 20 years later, it counted 800 exorcist members and 120 auxiliaries. Before becoming an exorcist at the age of 60, he worked as a journalist. Over his lifetime, he wrote numerous books and hosted a popular radio program on Radio Maria in Rome.

Did this book help you in some way? If so, I'd love to hear about it. Sincere reviews on **Amazon** and **Goodreads** help readers find the right book they are looking for.

Made in the USA
Las Vegas, NV
25 August 2023

76597767R00059